Crisis Therapy

Guidelines for the Practice
of
Crisis Intervention

by

Joseph B. France, M.S.W., M.P.H.

International Society for General Semantics
San Francisco

Crisis Therapy

International Society for General Semantics
L.C.C.C. No. 80-83967
ISBN 0-918970-28-8

Acknowledgements

The late Lydia Rapoport, formerly of the University of California, Berkeley, School of Social Welfare, opened up for me the practice of crisis intervention.

Lucy Loftis of the American National Red Cross furthered the application and practice of my ideas.

Maura Carroll, School of Nursing, University of California in San Francisco, was a source of inspiration and challenge.

*   *   *   *   *

I wish to thank M. H. E. Appley for permission to reprint the excerpt from his book, *Psychological Stress*.

To the baby and to my parents for their love.
J. B. F.

Table of Contents

Introduction 1

Section I —

The Knowledge Base for Crisis Therapy .. 7

Definitions of stress, crisis, threat, coping, forms of coping, personality and behavior.

Section II —

Assessment for Crisis Therapy 23

Assessment based upon the individual's environment, beliefs, values, sense of self, social and maintenance systems, network and role behavior, role performance, subculture, involuntary loss, basic needs, expected wants, transition and choice. Assessment in the first interview, modification, thought and the assessment process, cognition, identification of the problem, scope and duration of the problem, time.

Section III —

The Process of Crisis Therapy 53

Short-term therapy, goals of therapy, objectives of the goals, therapy, the therapist's goals, the therapeutic dialogue, risk-taking, what how and why questions, focus, catharsis, emotion and past experiences, defensiveness, respite and crisis, the captive and involuntary client, crisis and aggression, roles of the therapist, problem-solving, termination, guidelines for the therapist, operating procedures for the client, crisis from illness and the helping professions.

Introduction

BEGINNING IN THE 1960s the helping professions developed a new service which is best described as crisis intervention. This was a service through which the professions have been able to offer help for the problems of individuals and families in a situation of high risk because of threat or stress stemming from the problems they encounter in life.

Establishment of this service is a significant step, for it represents recognition by the helping professions that many people can not cope with the stress and threats of living in today's society, and as a result they enter a state of crisis.

The need the helping professions perceived and answered in the 1960s is even more acute in the 1980s.

The following example clearly indicates the need for a method of therapy directed toward crisis:

An elderly, gray-haired woman walked into the restroom of a downtown bus terminal, swallowed some poison pills, and sat on a bench until she died. She left the following note:

> "I'm sorry I had to do this but I have not a cent to eat on, no place to live. I thought maybe I

could get some work but it seems like I could not. I have not one relative left.

"I had a nephew who died about two months ago in Canada, which leaves me all alone. No money to bury me, so please just bury me as cheap as you can or cremate and put in ocean. Please, I feel awfully sorry about this, but God will bless who in the City will take care of it. I have been so hungry for two days and I can not stand it any longer and I do not know where to go. Thanks."

The note in her purse was not made public. The coroner discreetly placed it in her file; because she was alone in a public place, had no identification and would never be missed, that file is still headed, "Jane Doe No. 6."

Jane Doe was not writing about suicide. Instead, she listed stresses for which she saw no solution. Those overwhelming external stresses and their emotional aspects placed her in a state of crisis. Her answer to this, in her manner of thinking, was suicide.

Crisis can become the terminal state of people who are so troubled, angry or sad, or who are so ill from social conditions that they finally despair of coping — and therefore of living.

Not all people who experience crisis, of course, find their solution in suicide. Many seek out professional services. But, if the wrong kind of help is offered during an individual's struggle with crisis, the result can be disaster.

Originally crisis intervention was primarily the work of psychiatric social workers, psychiatric nurses, psychiatric aides, psychologists and psychiatrists. However, the number and types of people experiencing crisis have increased, and they have sought help from different service systems. Today crisis intervention programs have become more identified by their types; suicide, alcoholism, drug abuse, rape, battered women, child abuse, single parent families, and these services are offered by many different public and private groups.

Service systems dealing with the captive (public welfare) and involuntary (probation, parole) client have also increasingly encountered crisis situations.

However, the professionals who are faced with crises are often confused as to what the guidelines are for good practice with difficult problems. This confusion comes from differences between the concepts and clinical practice of traditional psychotherapy and the concepts and clinical practice of crisis therapy. The differences between these two forms of therapy require that the practitioner understand the different basics and have command of clinical skills which are appropriate to each.

For example, a major change between traditional therapy and crisis therapy is in the source of the causation — what caused the person to have this problem now? Traditional psychotherapy considers causation primarily from a historical psychological development of personality. Crisis therapy considers causation from an assessment of the individual's current socio-psychological functioning as related to his current circumstances — his immediate environment. This reconsideration of the causes and the implementation of appropriate therapy techniques are major changes for most of the helping professions.

The purpose of this book is to ensure that people in crisis receive appropriate service — crisis intervention.

This book develops and explains guidelines for use in all helping services which are concerned with individuals in crisis. The knowledge base which supports crisis therapy is developed from theories of stress, threat, coping and crisis. It presents a clinical model for assessment and treatment of the individual based upon knowledge from social work, social psychology and sociology.

The author has purposely not used detailed clinical case examples. The established practice of teaching by the case method is limited in its usefulness in most crisis situations. For professionals to learn

from case examples, three factors must be present:
1. An understanding of the organizational structure of a service system,
2. A description of the education and experience of the therapist,
3. A clinical description and assessment of the client in his environment.

The need of the client, and the state of preparedness of the therapist to help the client meet that need, are equally important. The client is not considered alone. This book is written for students of all the helping professions, for the "front-line" practitioner and for all self-help groups. The book, however, is not just a "how-to" model. This model requires a judgment on the part of the practitioner as to when, and with whom, it can be used. The disciplined thinking and the abilities necessary to practice the model can be learned.

1
The Knowledge Base For Crisis Therapy

THE PRACTICE OF crisis therapy introduces the professional to a different knowledge base. It has existed for some time, but in many settings it is still unknown. One of the major reasons for this is that the knowledge base has never been presented in a manner easily understood or in a form clearly related to practice. The major concepts come from socio-psychological understanding of stress, threat, coping, personality and behavior.

STRESS

Stress is inherent in the environment of day-to-day living and is also necessary for an individual's growth and development throughout life. As the individual responds to the self, to others and to the culture, he inevitably experiences stress. However, he may not recognize it as such because of its positive feature of moving the individual through the process of living.

Stress is the rate of growth, change, wear and tear

within the individual as he functions within his environment. Pelletier describes daily stress as follows:

Following a stressful day, your entire physiology is likely to be functioning as though your life were in danger. But since there is actually no immediate threat to your life, there is little opportunity to identify and recover from any particular source of stress. Most of our daily threats are ambiguous, and this prevents a significant recovery from the stress-alarm reaction which they induce. This prolonged unabated stress from which the individual has no respite is primarily responsible for the development of stress-related disorders.[1]

Pelletier points out that, ". . . stress-induced disorders have long since replaced epidemics of infectious disease as the major medical problem of the postindustrial nations."[2] So life naturally produces stressful and threatening situations from which there must be some form of release. However, whenever the degree of stress or threat in living becomes greater than the relief that is available, tension or depression results.

Stress may arise from circumstances over which the individual has limited control, such as the cost of food, clothing and shelter. It may also be related directly to that aspect of the individual's lifestyle which he can control, such as the person with whom he lives, or how much he drinks. The individual's lifestyle determines the kind and the intensity of the stress encountered. The migrant farm worker, the advertising executive and the teenage parent of a battered child manifest stress differently.

Stress is also cumulative in nature. As a person moves through life, he is vulnerable not only to his own aspirations and limitations, but also to a society that fulfills or denies his needs. The slow cumulative nature of stress means that some problems never become a crisis, but this does not mean that they are ever really resolved. The individual lives with them, and his emotional and thinking responses to the stress they engender often persist after the problem situation has passed. It becomes part of the person's history of accumulative stress. In this manner, accumulative stress distorts other experiences; the external situation changes but the feelings and understandings remain unresolved.

Appley and Trumbull have considered the different aspects and spheres of stress:

1. Stress is probably best conceived as a state of the total organism under extenuating circumstances rather than as an event in the environment.

2. A great variety of different environmental conditions is capable of producing a stress state.
3. Different individuals respond to the same conditions in different ways. Some enter rapidly into a stress state, others show increased alertness and apparently improved performance, and still others appear to be "immune" to the stress-producing qualities of the environmental conditions.
4. The same individual may enter into a stress state in response to one presumably stressful condition and not another.
5. Consistent intraindividual, but varied interindividual psychobiological response patterns occur in stress situations. The notion of a common stress reaction needs to be reassessed.
6. The behaviors resulting from operations intended to induce stress may be the same or different, depending on the context of the situation and its induction.
7. The intensity and the extent of the stress state, and the associated behaviors, may not be readily predicted from a knowledge of the stimulus conditions alone, but require an analysis of underlying motivational patterns

and of the context in which the stress is applied.

8. Temporal factors may determine the significance of a given stressor and thus the intensity and extent of the stress state and the optimum measurement of effect.[3]

Situations of stress require coping; but it is seldom clear whether an individual's vulnerability to a crisis derives from stress over which he has limited awareness and little control; from his perception of the problem; from his failure to cope with the problem; or whether it is from all three combined. If what the individual does to cope with the situation is successful — from his perspective — then the stress or threat is overcome. If the coping is unsuccessful in his eyes, then he enters a condition of "at-risk" which can be the beginning of a crisis state.

The common feature of all crises is that the stress of a problem increases until it takes control of the individual.

CRISIS

The word "crisis" is commonly used in a loose manner to cover a multitude of situations. It is often used in situations of strong emotion to indicate the drama and the immediacy of the situation. For our purpose, a crisis is a situation where there is a definite threat, or an accumulation of stress, at or near the limit of a person's ability to cope.

The literature recognizes five essential features of a crisis, which Miller and Iscoe summarize as follows:

> *Time*. Crises are acute rather than chronic. They may be very brief or may last for lengthy periods.

> *Behavior change*. The individual in crisis is less effective than usual. His activity is related to an attempt to discharge internal tensions. There are successive abortive, trial-and-error attempts to solve the problem without apparent success. Constructive behavior decreases and frustration mounts.

> *Subjective aspects*. The person in crisis has feelings of helplessness and ineffectiveness as he is faced with what appear to be insoluble problems. His perception is colored by anxiety, fear, guilt and psychological defense reactions.

> *Relativistic aspects*. The individual perceives the crisis as an experience unique to him.

> *Organismic tension*. The person in crisis experiences generalized physical tension which may be expressed in a variety of symptoms, including those commonly associated with

anxiety. These reactions may be immediate and temporary, or they may constitute a long-term adjustment to the crisis situation itself.[4]

There are a number of other definitions of crisis; all of them recognize crisis as a turning point in the process of living — a turning point where there is a decisive change affecting the individual for better or for worse. While providing an opportunity for transition, this change also poses the danger of becoming self-perpetuating. The individual's sense of balance in life before and after the crisis is generally not the same.

The most significant definition comes from the individual's experiencing the stress of the crisis. It is the individual who decides whether he is in stress, and why it is a crisis. To the individual, stress and crisis generally consist of situations that affect his security.

Stress situations which often result in crisis are ones that the individual:

1. believes he can not handle satisfactorily,
2. can not avoid, although he sees the threat,
3. thinks are novel and unique to him,
4. may not identify specifically as a crisis, although he may identify overwhelming feelings,
5. generally has advance feelings of stress.[5]

THREAT

Crisis results not only from stress, but from threat as well. Threat is conceptually different from stress in that it results from anticipation of a future event on the basis of cues provided by a present situation. A threat varies, depending on what the threatened person thinks the future situation will do to him. The individual's vulnerability to threat increases with the amount of threat he perceives. A person may not recognize or may only partially recognize what actually exists; he may also be so hypervigilant that he perceives a greater threat than actually exists. The individual in crisis from threat may not have actually encountered the threatening situation. The fear of the threat can be sufficient. An animal's natural response to a threat is flight or fight; human beings, being animals, also have this natural response. Because of our social structure, however, humans do not often have the option of flight; we usually come to the conclusion that neither option is practicable.

Therefore, crisis can result from stress, cumulative stress, multifaceted stress, acute stress or threat.

COPING

The success of stress, threat and crisis intervention hinges upon successful coping — the focus of therapy. *Coping* here means controlling at least some part of the problem by maintaining the individual's habitual ways of doing things while solutions to the problem are being considered. It is an attempt to resolve conflict, reduce anxiety, remove a threat and preserve self-esteem. It means that the person encountering stress, threat or crisis must process the experience so that it does not accumulate and continue as an unresolved problem.

The processing of the situation is both cognitive (thinking) and affective (feeling). Its success varies according to:

1. the amount of time the individual is willing to give the situation,
2. the individual's native ability to understand,
3. the individual's current needs for security and the ability to risk doing something,
4. the availability of positive alternatives,
5. the possibility of success.

Coping does not necessarily mean achieving a permanent solution. It can mean compromise. It can mean resolution of and accommodation to the situation. Coping is an on-going process that is required for dealing with development and change throughout life. It involves acquisition of experience through which a person develops memories and thereby establishes a pattern of coping — a pattern that attempts to deal with change. Success in developing such a pattern varies. The environment simply happens to some people, while some learn to control it; with others, some part of the environment is always seen as threatening.

FORMS OF COPING

Successful coping processes are not the same for all situations. Different coping processes are required in different situations — threat, frustration, challenge or gratification. Lazarus identifies coping as direct action which is adaptive, or as defensive adjustment — which is not adaptive.

The direct actions are:
1. preparation against harm
2. attack
3. avoidance
4. inaction.[6]

Inaction is a coping strategy that is used only when there is no positive alternative. Alternatives that are considered negative appear to offer no choice. A wide range of alternatives offers freedom of choice, but the net result may be to leave one trapped in freedom — that is, not being able to make a choice of action.

Nonadaptive forms of coping are defensive adjustments, which are rationalization or denial; these may or may not allow some degree of correct awareness.

Such adjustments may be a self-dosing process, by which the individual deals with what he can; it may also constitute an attempt to eliminate part or all of the problem situation. Since defenses may be costly to the individual, they need to be evaluated according to:

1. how much effort is required to maintain self-deception in the light of contradictory evidence,
2. whether distortion of the situation results in faulty decisions,
3. whether the defense actually increases the individual's vulnerability to present and future stress and threat.

PERSONALITY AND BEHAVIOR IN STRESS AND CRISIS

It is necessary to differentiate between *personality* and *behavior* and formulate a working definition of each. *Personality* is the more enduring and complicated intrapsychic and intrapersonal process which is in continual development and change throughout life; it is the basis of behavior.

Allport defined personality as ". . . the dynamic organization within the individual of those psychological systems that determine unique adjustments to the person's environment."[7]

Observable behavior in response to a given situation does differentiate one person from another, but it does not constitute the personality itself — it only reflects the personality. The behaviors that indicate personality are consistent, repetitious and durable. They are capable of reappearing and are therefore stable dispositions. They act on and influence the individual's behavior adaptation, for they appear more readily than other forms of behavior; they are repeated under even unfavorable conditions.

Behavior resulting from stress, threat or crisis is not an expression of the total personality; therefore, it may or may not indicate usual ways of coping.

Caplan points out that crises produce behavior that is an attempt to protect the individual from threatening reality, and it may be an appropriate or an inappropriate temporary response.[8] That a behavior is considered abnormal, Kaplan and Langsley point out, is not sufficient reason to treat it during crisis.[9]

This does not mean that personality should be ignored. Instead of beginning with personality, crisis therapy begins with the individual's environment and determines what is positive and what is negative about his functioning in that particular environment.

STRESS OR THREAT THAT CAN LEAD TO CRISIS

For stress or threat to be understood, an appraisal of the situation must be made. For an appraisal to be effective, the situation must be correctly perceived.

Every situation of stress and threat, however, has some degree of ambiguity or incomplete knowledge of the situation accentuated by defenses that deny some of the reality of the situation.

These factors can eventually increase the intensity of the stress/threat. In order to cope with the situation, the individual uses coping processes that have been used in the past. The greater the stress/threat, the more desparate will be the use of coping strategies. Coping requires not only psychological resources but also the ability and knowledge required to use them.

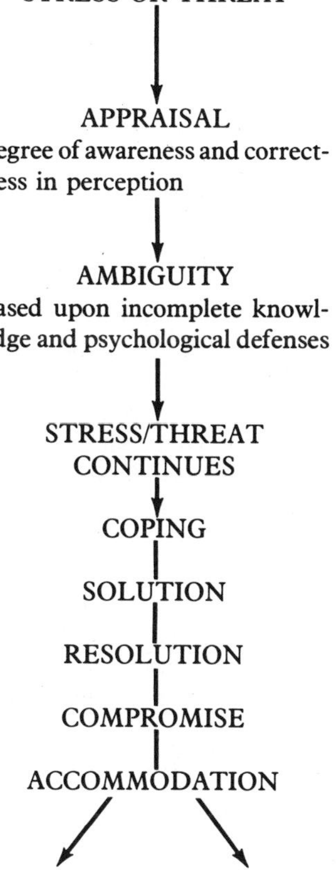

Figure 1.

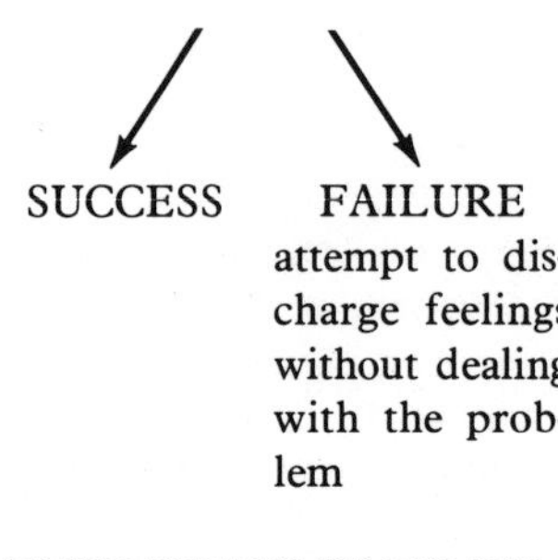

When coping is unsuccessful, emergency problem-solving strategies may be used.

If none of these emergency strategies is used, the person continues in the condition and enters an impasse in which he does not know what to do or what to think, or whether his feelings and thoughts are correct.

Nonadaptive defenses, self-devaluation and sense of stigma follow the crisis situation if intervention is not successful.

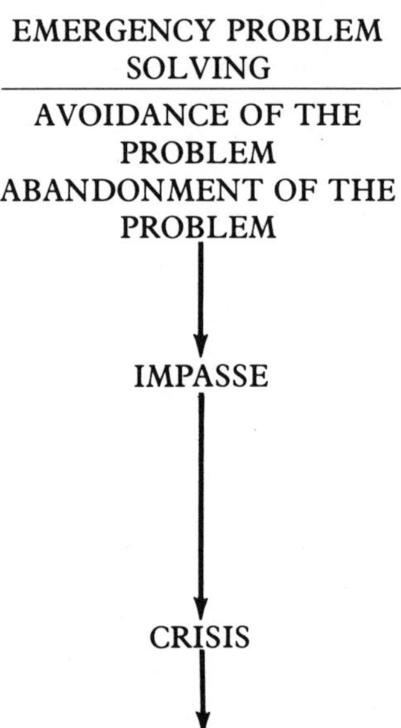

Figure 1. (cont.)

1. Pelletier, Kenneth *Mind as Healer, Mind as Slayer*, New York, Dell Publishing Co., 1977, p 241.
2. Pelletier, Kenneth *op. cit.*, p 242
3. Appley, M H E and Trumbull, R *Psychological Stress*, New York, Appleton-Century-Crofts, 1967.
4. Miller, K and Iscoe, I "The Concept of Crisis: Current Status and Mental Health Implications," *Human Organization*, vol. 22, 1968, p 146.
5. Lazarus, Richard *Psychological Stress and the Coping Process*, New York, McGraw-Hill Book Co., 1966, p 222.
6. Lazarus, Richard *op. cit.*, p 262.
7. Allport, Gordon *Personality: A Psychological Interpretation*, New York, H. Holt & Co., 1937, p 48.
8. Caplan, Gerald *Principles of Preventive Psychiatry*, New York, Basic Books, Inc., 1964, p 112.
9. Langsley, Donald G., and Kaplan, David M. *The Treatment of Families in Crisis*, New York, Grune and Stratton, 1960, p 25.

2
Assessment For Crisis Therapy

ASSESSMENT, AS USED here, means a knowledgeable opinion that results from disciplined thinking. Assessment is directed to the conscious processes of thinking and feeling as they relate to a problem situation and to the client's behavior in a particular environment.

The implementation of assessment requires the therapist to be aware that individuals live within a network of interlocking and interdependent environmental systems. These environments form a network of connections which comprises the reality within which the individual experiences the process of life. The constant interaction of these systems requires that the individual balance the entire network — by coping.

The individual's network of environmental systems is presented in Figure 2. This figure represents major systems of an individual's life, regardless of age, sex or race. In short, all individuals have a similar network.

THE INDIVIDUAL'S ENVIRONMENTAL NETWORK
System of American cultural beliefs: masculinity, femininity, God, country, etc.
System of institutions: science, technology, media, urbanization, mechanization
SUBCULTURAL SYSTEM
Sense of Self System
Role functions
Peer acceptance
Self-acceptance
Family acceptance
Values
Beliefs
Social approval
Social System
Religion
Love
Sex
Drugs
Standards of Morality
Life-Style System
Needs
Wants
Transitions
Losses
Degree of upward or downward mobility
System of constraints
Physical
Biological
Social
Economic
Maintenance System
Money
Job
Health
Illness
Age
Education
Motivational System
Expectations
Safety
Danger
Failure
Success
Ability to risk in life
Cognitive System
Knowledge
Thinking
Reasoning
Memory
Recall

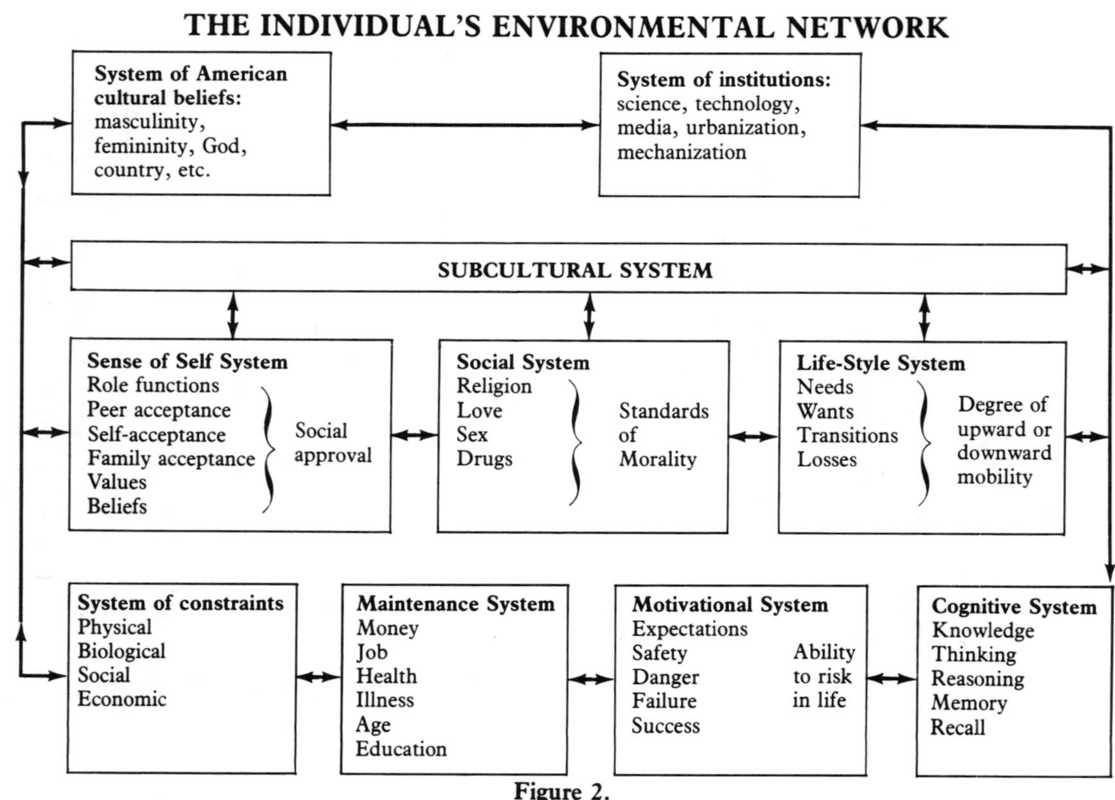

Figure 2.

In the assessment process the therapist considers the interaction of the environmental network through an understanding of: beliefs and values, the sense of self, social and maintenance systems, network and role behavior, and subculture. The therapist's understanding of these factors and their interaction is important. Understanding the environmental network is the major guideline that asks, "Where is the crisis? How does it affect the individual's present life?"

Individuals can experience a crisis that affects only part of their network of environments, e.g., a low sense of self, but at the same time holding a satisfying job. It is important to determine what areas are affected and which areas can help the person to cope.

BELIEFS AND VALUES

What a person has in life, what he considers to be important, and what he wants in life are a reflection of cultural and individual beliefs and values.

Beliefs determine both objectives and goals for the individuals' life. A belief results in motivation to do something, for it establishes norms and sets expectations. Although beliefs are learned early in life, the individual eventually develops a degree of independence from the previous learning, which rearranges what the individual believes and values.

Values give the individual's beliefs a hierarchical organization, for they are the conventions that allow prejudgment to be made. Both are activated by situations, events, people, and they are an important part of coping in a society with many different beliefs and values.

Beliefs and values can be expressed cognitively through knowledge, affectively through intensity, and behaviorally through action. They are a part of the individual's "rights in life" because they save time by providing an immediate standard. How many beliefs and values an individual has indicates the flexibility and/or rigidity of the conscious mind, for it indicates the number and types of different thoughts which the individual can consider. Flexibility and/or rigidity of the conscious mind is also a coping ability.

THE SENSE OF SELF

Life requires that we learn, through the resolution of problems, to cope, to adapt and to change. It is a process commonly referred to as maturing; Erickson refers to it as a sense of wholeness.[1]

The key to this process is the sense of *self*. As the individual has beliefs and values toward the world around him, so he has beliefs and values about himself. These constitute the conscious aspects of personality and are described as the sense of self.

When exposed to the stress of life, and especially when in a crisis state, the individual experiences assaults on his sense of self. A crisis involving the sense of self often involves a clash between the individual's evaluation of himself and the evaluation he wishes others to make. Life is a situation of continued stress involving defense of the self and acceptance of the self. Much has been written about this, and in terms of stress and crisis self-acceptance can be considered like the common cold.

Abilities that figure importantly in the sense of self are:

1. *Family and Peer Acceptance.* The ability to create and sustain interpersonal relationships that are based on warmth and sincerity and that involve giving and taking to meet the needs of self and others.

2. *Self-acceptance:* A self-image based on self-respect. It involves seeing and accepting who one is so that one can be what he presently is.

3. *Aspirations and Limitations:* The ability to develop goals, however limited, and the ability to postpone some gratification of impulses and to tolerate the frustrations and other discomforts that come from delayed gratification or relinquishment of some goals.

4. *Role Functions:* The emotional energy sufficient to meet one's own personal needs and to
meet the needs of others by pursuing a job,
a career, a family or causes.

SOCIAL AND MAINTENANCE SYSTEMS

Every individual lives within a social context in which people influence one another, and in which there are demands, pleasures, cooperation and conflicts. Szasz has stated, "The social situation in which the person lives constitutes the team on which he plays and is important in determining who he is and how he acts."[2] From the team we derive a sense of belonging, a vital emotional support in the living, loving and working relationships.

These sources of support can help sustain the individual, but they can also be the source of stress. The most important influences on people are from those with whom they share their lives and to whose needs and individual personalities they must adapt. No individual therapist can ever have this kind of influence. The importance of the support that social and maintenance systems can provide during periods of crisis can be seen in the following case examples . . .

Georgette, a 25-year-old mother, brought her 5-year-old child into the emergency room of the local community hospital. The child, who had been accidentally shot by his 7-year-old brother, was pronounced dead. The police were called to investigate the situation and began to question the mother and child. Georgette was divorced and the father of her children had remarried and was living in another part of the country. They maintained no contact. She was new to the community and was acquainted with few people. Her only means of support was public welfare. She had a boyfriend who was occasionally employed, but she did not know where he was at this time. Upon completion of the police questioning, Georgette was allowed to go home with the other child, who kept saying, "I don't want to go to jail!"

Here a social network that could support the client was lacking. An astute nurse, however, arranged for the development of a social network by calling in a public health nurse. This nurse made visits to Georgette's home to provide support for her and possibly to develop other resources.

Gertrude was a 32-year-old divorcee who had remarried and had one child from the previous marriage. Her second husband was successful in business and well known in the community. She was happy with her second husband and became pregnant by him. One morning when Gertrude had gone back to bed, her child from the first marriage fell into the swimming pool. In the emergency room of the hospital he was pronounced dead. The attending doctor was most supportive, for he was a social acquaintance of Gertrude. Gertrude's husband was also at the hospital and was able to provide support. The police questioning was delayed. The couple left shortly afterward for a rest in Hawaii.

NETWORK AND ROLE BEHAVIOR

A person's life consists of a number of *roles* which comprise a network within which he functions. Each role is a part of the whole and contributes to the network of roles which contributes to the sense-of-self system. The roles that are ascribed, such as male, female, son, daughter, we take for granted; however, the ascribed roles indicate to whom a person responds — such as to a mother or a father — and thus they can be a source of support and conflict. Other roles are achieved, such as employer and employee, and they require certain types of behavior for successful performance. Some roles, such as that of a parent, are usually held for a long time, whereas others, such as that of a soldier, often are temporary. All role behavior, whether ascribed or achieved, is governed by prescriptions that are sanctioned by society, but that vary from subculture to subculture.

The assumption of a role and the behavior necessary for functioning within that role are learned through the interaction of the individual with his culture and his fellow beings. The culture facilitates this process through the establishment and recognition of various roles, such as husband and parent. The roles that a person fulfills reflect the defined groups of society to which he relates. Because of the length of time required to learn roles and their values, they become one of the more permanent parts of an individual's identity; they become habitual.

Role behaviors are governed by the demands made upon the role-player by himself, by those with whom he interacts, by the subculture and the larger culture. Social interaction between individuals occurs in defined roles and in situations that are defined by roles. An example is the doctor-patient relationship. The predetermined boundaries of roles and the rules that govern the interaction of the role-players are sources of security.

Since most people's sense-of-self is based on the type, number and quality of the roles they assume, beliefs and sense-of-self are vulnerable to change when there is a change in role. Thus, dependence on roles for security and sense-of-self predisposes most individuals to intense stress. Changes in role behavior are generally difficult because they require, to some degree, a redefinition of the sense-of-self, a change in beliefs and a change in role behaviors, all of which place the individual in a novice role.

When a change in roles occurs, adaptation becomes especially important. Adaptation to a new role is not necessarily pleasurable, however, especially if the person does not have the necessary capacity for performance. The relinquishment of one role and the assumption of another require preparation, but preparation for a new role that is not assumed voluntarily causes intense stress. Each person wishes to achieve comfort and return through satisfaction in his role behavior, but these are qualities which cannot be guaranteed. Stress, threat and crisis in role behavior can become chronic and demoralizing, resulting in a loss of self-esteem, confusion and personal immobilization — a sense of, "What do I do when there is nothing I am willing to change?"

Role performance or the acceptance of a new role can be explored by analyzing four considerations:

1. *Role Expectation.* What is the performance that the individual thinks is necessary? Does the person have the necessary information to understand whether his expectations are correct?

2. *Role Concept.* What does the person think will be the effect of the role on his sense-of-self? (This is the affective aspect of role performance.)

3. *Role Acceptance.* How well does the person accept the role? If a new role is being forced on him by outside pressures, there will always be an unwillingness to change because of the fear of the unknown.

4. *Role Performance.* What is the degree of the individual's success in performing his present role? Is this satisfactory in the individual's opinion? What is the possibility of the person's success in performing a new role? Successful role performance depends on all the preceding three considerations.

SUBCULTURE

A single, society-wide set of norms for behavior is generally considered to exist. The United States, however, is a heterogeneous and socially differentiated culture, and norms differ according to socio-economic level, geographic area, degree of urbanization, ethnic group, race and sex.

Normative homogeneity probably only exists in the buying of products and services, for we all have the same physical needs and we all need certain services to function in the larger society. This economic homogeneity cannot be equated with psycho-social homogeneity.

We are born into a subculture, but as adults we

can also choose another subculture. We as individuals can have more behavioral variation from one subculture to another than any other species because we can both adapt to and create a subculture. The socialization of the individual to one or more subcultures is an on-going process — the person who at one time "dropped out" and joined a commune may now be working on Wall Street. These processes of change themselves create a situation of stress.

The subculture offers a range of options that both constrains and at the same time is an expression of individual behavior — but, it does not dictate the choice. The choice is determined by a consideration of opportunities, demands and private thoughts and emotions. The choice that is made is not necessarily conforming or deviant because the subculture's norms are frequently vague and variations are therefore tolerated.

However, in assessment it is also important to understand what the situation means to the individual in the process of living. This part of the assessment is based upon a consideration of what the crisis is doing to the individual's entire life — now and in the future. In what way may the individual's life be altered?

There are three major types of stress which can result in a crisis and an alteration of the individual's life:

STRESS OF INVOLUNTARY LOSS

In a society where a high value is placed on winning, and where winning is supposed to represent security, loss or losing has an especially strong impact on the loser. Loss involves the evaluation and the development of a new form of dependency, one in which there may be less to be dependent upon and little hope that what has been lost will be recovered. Because the stress of loss affects the satisfactions that the individual has been experiencing in life, the individual must develop a new and satisfactory balance.

Understanding the stress of loss entails these questions:

> *What type of security or satisfaction is lost?* Money, freedom, health, job, lover, home, sex?
>
> *When does the loss occur during the life span of the person?* Some losses are less difficult to accept at one time of life than at another. The loss of a job by a 55-year-old person is different from the loss of a job by a 25-year-old person. The loss of a breast by a 70-year-old woman is different from the same loss by a 40-year-old woman.
>
> *How did the loss occur?* The loss may occur in such a way that it is taken as an unflattering reflec-

tion upon the loser. Goffman describes this well:

"A person may be involuntarily deprived of a role under circumstances which reflect unfavorably on his capacity for it. The lost role may be one that he had already acquired, or one that he openly committed himself to preparing for. In either case, the loss is more than a matter of ceasing to act in a given capacity; it is ultimate proof of an incapacity. And in many cases it is even more than this. The moment of failure often catches a person acting as one who feels that he is an appropriate sort of person for the role in question."[3]

The person who experiences an involuntary loss may believe that the real cause lies within himself. People who suffer from loss grow weary of blaming themselves, and when their sense-of-self in effect says, "I've had enough of blaming myself!" they then blame others. These forms of coping are not adaptive. They constitute an attempt to discharge feelings, but in fact they only increase the vicious circle of self-blame and blame of others. The use of emotional energy in this manner leaves the person feeling incompetent to make necessary changes or otherwise cope with the situation.

BASIC NEEDS/EXPECTED WANTS STRESS

In these crises the individual perceives the situation as depriving him of basic needs or expected wants in life. It is a difference between what the individual has, what he needs and what he expects.

What is perceived as a need versus a want is based upon the individual's perception of what is available to him and what should be available. His inability to attain what he wants in life increases his feelings of isolation based on failure. It results in a unique feeling that the individual is a minority of one, for both the expectation and the opportunity to fulfill the expectation are gone.

Individual needs and expected wants do change; the person changes with age and his preferences and expectations change. The more basic the need and the more important the threatened want, the greater the sense of stress. Need/Want stress may result from surrender to the realization that what has been seen as a want is, in fact, a satisfaction that may never be attained. An individual's failure to satisfy what he has always considered to be a want, and his inability to have what his upbringing has taught him to expect, may precipitate a crisis.

STRESS OF TRANSITION AND CHOICE

Another type of stress occurs during the process

of maturing: the stress of *transition*. This stress can include entering school, reaching adolescence, leaving school, getting a job, losing a job, getting married, having a baby, separating, divorcing, remarryig or cohabitation, suffering chronic or acute major illness or surgery, reorganizing the family, undergoing climacteric, entering retirement, aging and dying.

That stress leading to crisis commonly accompanies these transitional events is often overlooked precisely because almost everyone experiences them. These stresses also arise because individuals cannot understand and/or control all the processes that affect their lives.

Transition stress is a primary example of the developmental nature of life. Erikson describes the sequence of adult development as ". . . intimacy vs isolation; generativity vs stagnation; integrity vs despair."[4]

The stress, threat and crisis of transitions is not whether a person will undergo transition as a developmental part of life, but under what conditions it occurs. Transitional stress involves the balance of frustration, gratification, stimulation and security in life. Levinson identifies nine transitions which the individual must cope with over the years.[5] Each period involves a reconsideration of the individual's dependency in life — dependency based upon the self and dependency based upon others.

Transitional stress often forces the individual to consider questions which are basic for reappraisal: where one has come from — experience, where one is now; what one still dreams of — the quality of hope. Levinson describes this as the degree of illusion in life vs the degree of disillusionment in life.[6]

Transitions in life involve a consideration of what the individual has created, what is missing, what is wrong and what works. In assessment the evaluation also considers the prospect of future possibilities and the types of *choice* which can be made to reach short- and long-term objectives. Choice indicates the possibility of alternatives, which brings into consideration the consequence of choice. Choice in life is not easy, for there are no "Good Housekeeping Seals of Approval." To make a choice means participation through which the individual becomes involved and committed to someone, some group, some thing, some objective or goal — or conversely, does not become involved or committed.

Individuals are always in the process of transition, which has both negative and positive features. The transitions from the negative to the positive, however, generally involve the attainment of something the individual deserves. Transitions from the positive to the negative involve a surrender that makes the process more noticeable and therefore more painful.

ASSESSMENT IN THE FIRST INTERVIEW

In the first interview, assessment is based upon a synthesis of the client's thinking and emotional processes as evidenced by his words, emotions and behaviors.

First considered is the client's condition; is he depressed? Does he present a problem which overwhelms him? The presenting condition indicates the initial approach that the therapist should take. A crisis involving divorce, for instance, may be first presented as depression over loss, or it may be presented as a problem about what to do about building a new life, or a new identity, this latter being more of a cognitive quality.

Generally, in making the assessment, the therapist has to alternate between affective and cognitive approaches to see which elicits a response that seems more amenable to consideration. For example, when a client is in a state of depression, even a limited new perspective may spark a sense of hope that the situation can be resolved. The key factor in this process is that the therapist must have some understanding and must begin to convey that quality.

In making an assessment the therapist must evaluate what the client presents in order to develop hypotheses which are the beginning of action. The hypotheses consider the client's relationship to his environmental network. They clarify what the problem is and the nature of its cause and effects. The forming of hypotheses in assessment is a process based upon an exchange of talking, listening and feeling. The therapist offers help on the basis of what he understands. From this an estimation is developed of how the situation may be *modified*.

MODIFICATION

Modification considers:
1. How many stresses or threats are present?
2. What change is needed? Changes may be required in the client's understanding of the situation, his emotional reaction to it, or external factors.
3. To what extent can the situation be changed? What are the client's resources? Who or what exists within his environment that could help? Who or what within the client's environment hinders the modification?
4. What means are available for change?

In considering the possibilities for modification, the therapist must determine the specifics of the situation and must not trust verbal generalizations.

THOUGHT AND
THE ASSESSMENT PROCESS

In the assessment process the therapist's efforts are focused only on the directed thought of the client. "Directed thought is conscious, i.e. it pursues an aim in the mind of the thinker; it is intelligent, which means that it is adapted to reality and tries to influence it; it admits of being true or false (empirically or logically true) and it can be communicated by language."[7]

It is important that the therapist not focus on the undirected thoughts of his client. Undirected thought ". . . is subconscious, which means that the aim it pursues and the problems it tries to solve are not present in consciousness; it is not adapted to reality, but creates for itself a dream world of imagination; it tends not to establish truths, but to satisfy desires and it remains strictly individual and incommunicable as such by means of language."[8]

In crisis situations the individual can be so upset that undirected thought can be very apparent, but a focus upon undirected thought is not appropriate for crisis therapy.

COGNITION

Cognition here refers to the conscious functions of the mind: knowing, thinking, reasoning, remembering and problem-solving, all of which are processes of coping.

The emotional nature of stress, threat and crisis situations narrows these abilities and adds confusion and distortion to the situation; but the quality of thought and the thinking abilities of the individual are most important. Cognition involves an interaction between the individual and the environment as he attempts to understand and make the necessary accommodation to maintain balance. The better the individual understands his situation, the more incentive he will have to control some part of it.

Susan Sontag describes this as, "An awful lot of feeling that seems just like feeling ends up with being passive, feeling that you can't change things; whereas what feels like thinking seems like the beginning of some kind of control, or intervention."[9]

Cognition is the learning aspect of therapy. A crisis is often a new experience for the person, as is therapy that is directed toward resolution of the problem. Although some understanding of the situation is basic for its resolution, the person will not have complete knowledge of his situation, for it is difficult to know all one needs to know about the variables affecting one's life. The therapist's sharing of his knowledge and perspective with the client is an important part of the therapy. Change often depends upon knowledge that gives more perspective.

Cognition is not an independently rational, adoptive process. The client's knowledge of the situation will be colored by his values and beliefs, and his motivations and thoughts, through which he evaluates expectations, and demands and chooses a course of action.

IDENTIFICATION OF THE CRISIS

When the overwhelming emotions of the crisis have been somewhat defused, the assessment for therapy moves toward a clearer identification and definition of the problem. Clear identification is an important part of assessment because it develops a consideration of present and future . . . Where are we? Where do we go? The more clearly the crisis can be defined, the easier it is to determine what constraints and alternatives are available. Here the therapist may encounter resistance, for to identify the problem is to change the focus from an emotional theme to its possible resolution. Many clients ask for help because their problems are painful, but they also resist help because the work of resolving their problems is also painful.

Identification of the nature of the crisis can be a difficult process because it is frequently hindered by extraneous factors. People have developed a sophistication about the helping services. They realize that in order to receive service, they must have the "right" problem — they identify the problem according to the service available. Others identify the problem according to how relevant the client believes the therapist considers the problem. And still others feel a cultural stigma is attached to an inability to handle personal problems; they present "respectable" problems, such as one involving money, as a screen.

The individual may be able to identify a crisis because it is more comfortable to have a problem that can be felt, identified and described. Abstract discomfort produces more anxiety and reduces the opportunity to blame events or other people.

But the client may not be able to identify a problem and he may be in an emotional state; this state is the presenting condition, but it is not the problem. Emotions can run the entire range, but they will generally have a primary feature, such as depression, anxiety or anger. Problems that result from an accumulation of the stress of living are the most difficult to pinpoint.

For a problem to exist, a situation may not actually threaten harm to the individual. He need only perceive that it may. What the individual perceives should not automatically be equated with what is tangible and verifiable. The therapist often cannot be sure at first whether the client is reacting to real things or imagined things. What he is reacting to must be ascertained, for this will determine what the therapist focuses upon: problems or feelings.

The identification of the problem should be based upon evidence — the sequence of events and the facts of the situation; this evidence should make sense to the individual and should be comprehensible to the therapist. In other words, the client's behavior, thoughts and feelings should be understood by both client and therapist so that they are seen as appropriate, to some degree, in the context of the client's situation.

In identifying the problem, the therapist may encounter one or more of these problems:

1. A problem exists but is not identified by either the client or the therapist.
2. The problem exists and is identified, but no solution is known to either the client or the therapist.
3. The problem exists and is identified; a solution is not known to the client but is known to the therapist.
4. The problem exists and is identified; the solution is known to the client but not to the therapist.

Once at least some aspect of the problem is identified, the assessment process can move to the dis-
covery of which aspects are amenable to immediate
relief; this is the initial objective of therapy.

In this problem-identification process the therapist looks for the possibility of the client to assume
responsibility over some part of the problem. However limited such responsibility may be, it is the first
step toward the reduction of blaming and complain-
ing, which are not positive forms of coping.

A case in point concerned a woman who sought
marital counseling from a therapist: She and her husband were separated, ostensibly because their personal living habits were in conflict. She wanted to
save everything, so that the home came to look like
a "rat's nest," whereas he wanted to throw everything out. Later the real problem became apparent
when the wife finally asked her husband, "Should
we tell the therapist?" The husband had leukemia
at age 35. In this situation, the future crisis (the
husband's death) was causing the present crisis. She
wanted to save everything so that she would lose less;
he was losing the most precious quality, and so to
him the other things were unimportant. That this
may appear obvious does not mean that it was obvious to either of the individuals involved.

SCOPE AND DURATION OF THE PROBLEM

The assessment process also consists of an evaluation of the *scope* of the problem. "Scope" here answers the question, Which of the various environmental systems are affected?

The stress may be long-standing and it may have affected numerous systems of functioning. Here it is important to understand how the person has coped with the problem and why that coping is not working now. To discern these differences and to contain the problem are other objectives of therapy. The *duration* of the problem is measured from the onset of the precipitating stress or the beginning of the threat; it is,

> ". . . any event in the development of an organism that interferes with the most efficient adaptation to a given environmental stress factor (or precipitating factor) that occurs later in the life of that organism."[10]

TIME

The element of time is an important consideration for both the client and the resolution of the problem.

Time affects the assessment, the process of therapy and the goals that have been determined. The very nature of a crisis situation challenges any previous time perspective. Now everything seems more immediate. Time puts pressure on the individual in crisis to receive some service that will resolve the problem; time exerts pressure on the therapist to make a decision about what to do and to make the right decision. Nevertheless, time in some length is necessary to resolve crisis. Often a person had to relearn a sense of time and what it means in this situation. Despite a client's feeling of urgency, crisis situations generally cannot be resolved immediately.

All the preceding factors are important in assessment. They are presented in Figure 3.

OUTLINE FOR THE ASSESSMENT OF INDIVIDUALS IN STRESS, THREAT AND CRISIS

1. **Precipitating stress or threat**

Known	Unknown
Acute	Cumulative or multidimensional

2. **Crisis problem**

Known	Unknown (the person in crisis will need to develop knowledge of what happened and how)

Figure 3.

3. **Scope**

   Single problem   Multiple problem

4. **Duration and time frame**

   How long has the problem situation existed?

5. **Present condition and functioning**

Cognitive	**Affective**
Thinking	Anxiety, free-floating or identified
Understanding	Depression, cause known or unknown
Reasoning	Guilt, realistic or unrealistic
Ability for problem solving	Anger toward person or situation

6. **Type of crisis**

   Involuntary loss
   Need — want
   Transition
   Other

7. **Area most affected**

   Physical health
   Food, clothing, shelter
   Beliefs, values
   Sense of self: self-acceptance, peer acceptance, family
   acceptance, aspirations, limitations
   Social network: social and maintenance systems
   Role performance: a change in role, or stress brought about
   by others' role performance

Figure 3 (cont.).

8. What in the crisis situation can be modified in a short-term intermediate objective?

9. What can the person do? To what extent? With what resources? What is the sequence of steps?

10. What is the person's ability and willingness to risk doing something about the crisis?

11. What is the possibility of developing coping ability?

    rapid   slow   not clear

12. What situational considerations support or inhibit coping and resolution?

Figure 3 (cont.).

REFERENCES

1. Erikson, E. *Identity Youth and Crises*, New York, W.W. Norton & Company, Inc., 1968, p 221.
2. Szasz, T. *The Ethics of Psychoanalysis; The Theory and Method of Autonomous Psychotherapy*, New York, Basic Books, 1965, p 71.
3. Goffman, E. "On Cooling the Mark Out," *Psychiatry: Interpersonal Process*, Vol. 15, No. 4, p 454.
4. Erikson, E. "Identity and the Life Cycle," *Psychological Issues*, No. 1 (1959), pp 1-171.
5. Levinson, D.J. *The Seasons of a Man's Life*, New York, Alfred A. Knopf, 1978.
6. Levinson, D.J. *op. cit.*, p 192.
7. Piaget, J. *The Language and Thought of the Child*, London, Routledge and Kegan Paul, 1926, p 63.
8. Piaget, J. *op. cit.*, p 64.
9. Drewes, C. Life and Death: A Conversation with Susan Sontag, *San Francisco Sunday Examiner and Chronicle*, March 28, 1978, p 2.
10. Brenner, M.H. *op. cit.*, p 7.

3
The Process Of Crisis Therapy

THE TREATMENT METHOD most appropriate for crisis is short-term therapy. The implication is not that stress, threat and crisis can always be resolved in a short time, but rather that the period during which the person is willing to face the situation and deal with it is limited.

Short-term therapy is not a new treatment method, but it has not been widely used because of the high value that has been attached to insight therapy — which, by its very nature, requires a long time. The attitude of the mental health professional toward short-term treatment has been described by Malan as ". . . the most easily identified tendency, as each new advance was made, has been towards an increase in the length of therapy. Thus anyone who tries to develop a technique of brief psychotherapy is trying to reverse an evolutionary process impelled by powerful forces."[1]

The negative attitude toward short-term therapy

is probably based upon an assumption that the results are not durable. Research, however, does not support this assumption. Reid and Shyre found that short-term treatment has yielded results ". . . at least as good as, and probably better than, open-ended treatment of longer duration."

A study by Langsley, Flomenhaft and Machotka investigated the results of two groups of 150 each. One group was admitted to the hospital and the other group was administered family crisis therapy on an outpatient basis. Six months after termination of treatment, the social and personal functioning levels of the two groups were not statistically significant. However, during the six-month posttreatment period, those who had been treated on an in-patient basis during the test period were readmitted to the hospital an average of 23 days; those who had remained in the community were hospitalized for an average of only five days. Those who avoided hospitalization in the first place were far more likely to avoid a later period of hospitalization than those who were initially admitted.[3]

The most successful criterion of therapy is not understanding, but successful performance. A person can be taught reasons for his problem, but that does not necessarily change the situation.

Wood, in an analysis of 22 studied on clinical practise, determined six principles of "quality practise."[4]

1. Accurate definition of the problem.
2. Analysis of the problem-factors creating or maintaining it and factors that can help resolve it.
3. Assessment of the problem's workability and setting the goals.
4. Negotiation of a contract with the client.
5. Planning a strategy of intervention.
6. Evaluation.

GOALS OF THERAPY

The shortness of time, the lowering of defenses, and the motivation to solve stress, threat and crisis, all call for moderate goals in therapy. Many goals are too ambitious, considering the limitation on the person, the situation, the therapist and service delivery system. Clients are often unwilling to invest enough effort in therapy to make it what the therapist considers a success. The professional emphasis on success often overlooks the practical goals that can be achieved. Short-term, limited-goal therapy can satisfy the acute needs of large numbers of people.

The goal of therapy must be to restore or develop functioning in a particular affected area. The therapist looks for realistic courses of action by determining what specific adaptations are possible for the client. It is important that the goals be established mutually, for if the therapist is to help the client, then the client should know how it is to be accomplished. A goal that is an adaptive resolution of the problem must make sense and be satisfactory to the client.

Determination of the goals begins in the first interview, with the client an active participant. The determination should take into account what the client should do, can do and will do. When considering goals, the client and the therapist compare their views to learn what the client thinks is most relevant. The therapist's function is to determine with the client the degree of fit between relevance and importance. The closer the fit, the greater the possibility for motivation of action.

Because the therapist's role is to help the client achieve what he wishes to achieve, or what he thinks he has to achieve, the goals set with the client do not need the approval of the therapist, nor does the therapist have to agree with them. However, it is incumbent on the therapist to consider whether any new problems are suggested by goals that the client proposes. These new problems can be pointed out as the goals are chosen. If the client still wishes to continue with the goals, the problems that may result from them can be considered.

Goals for the client and the objectives of the therapist are often confused, but they do differ. Goals for the client can be identified as affective, cognitive, situational-behavioral and situational:

- *Affective goals:* an ability to tolerate anxiety; an awareness of frustrations and tensions; the development of some sense of competence; a change in values and beliefs; the reduction of self-demands; the facilitation of catharsis.

- *Cognitive goals:* an increased understanding of the situation; assimilation of new information so that the client can begin to anticipate the future; an awareness of what the problem has meant to the client; a reconceptualization of the problem as a change rather than a loss; the reorganization of the information in the problem situation and how it is understood.

- *Situational-behavioral goals:* a change in some aspect of the subcultural network through a change in the social and maintenance systems; the removal of the client from the situation; supply of controls to enable the client to structure his time and activity.

- *Situational goals:* a redefinition of the problem; an alteration of expectations and demands on the life-style system; preparation for possible future problems.

Objectives of the goals:

1. The client should come to think that some aspect of the problem is within his control. He will then become more active in assessing and attempting to change the situation.
2. There should be a restoration of the coping abilities.
3. Active rather than passive coping should be restored or increased.
4. The problem should be kept from becoming chronic.

The achievement of any of these goals by the client eradicates the feelings of hopelessness; but if the problem is insoluble, now or in the future, feelings of hopelessness will increase and will cause other immediate problems. Situations that result in immediate and future problems require the development of goals for the client that are clearly distinguished as to their immediate and long-range focus. The difficulty in achieving long-range goals is that the client must incorporate information and experience about the past, present and future so that there is motivation and a plan for action. Planning without action is foolish, but action without planning is even more foolish.

Goals are in no respect neutral, for we all have beliefs and values that guide our thoughts. It is important that the therapist avoid requiring the client to adopt the therapist's values. Therapists often assume that their clients must cooperate fully — be a "good patient." The correct perspective is, however, that the therapist cooperate with the client. The client should receive a framework from the therapist that allows him to understand and to cope with the situation and possibly to transfer what he has learned from the therapy to other life problems.

THERAPY

Therapy means interaction between therapist and client that has meaning and purpose for the client. Meaningful interaction is not an isolated experience, but it exists on a continuum that constitutes the art of therapy. Therapy is a calculated and disciplined process in which the therapist makes contact with the client. A meaningful interaction is one that changes the client in some manner.

The therapeutic process described in this chapter does not necessarily involve the "ideal" client who is agreeable, responsive and open. In the process of therapy there is an unspoken conflict which consists of how much

- the therapist adjusts to the individual
- the individual adjusts to the therapist

Individuals in intense stress, threat and crisis are

often difficult people who live in a world separated from the therapist by income, education, social position, power and personal freedom — and with the problems related to each. Such clients tend to act and react before they think. Therapy must serve as a counterirritant to restore coping through understanding and reducing emotional tension. The first consideration is to deal with the irritant. The second is to reach a state of comfort in which the irritant is removed, if possible.

Therapy is a planned helping experience that should enable the client to pass a difficult point in life. It requires an immediate focus on the client and on his problem. The touchstone of therapy is the flexibility of the therapist. Each client presents the therapist with a combination of problems. Both the therapist and the client are engaged in a learning experience that is a cooperative enterprise. The therapist must draw upon his personal and professional experiences, utilize his education, and have empathy, objectivity, sensitivity and especially a willingness to learn. Here, the client is as useful to the therapist as the therapist is to the client.

THE THERAPIST'S GOAL

The role of the therapist is defined by professional education, by experience and by the work setting.

The client enters the therapy with a shattered sense of security. The therapist must convey comfort and security. The therapist's self-confidence can begin the renewal of the client's confidence. The sincerity of the relationship will develop through trust, respect and liking. The therapist's manner should convey attention and interest. This helps the client to begin communication in a situation that is difficult, for he will probably not know what is expected of him or what to expect of therapy. In addition to having to explain and justify thoughts and feelings, the client must develop a new relationship with a stranger. In such a context, the passive therapist who only asks questions, who remains uninvolved and unshockable, and who meanwhile makes close observations of the client, increases the client's anxiety and his wish to escape. If the therapist's style is to listen and not to talk, the client may think that the therapist is not interested in his problem. It may be difficult for the client to establish or maintain eye contact with the therapist.

It must not be assumed that once the techniques of therapy are mastered the job of the therapist will be easy. Therapists often forget that the basic techniques of therapy are to be there — talking, listening and, above all, being human.

THE THERAPEUTIC DIALOGUE

The therapeutic dialogue begins with communication about the problem; this is the first risk the client takes. In general, when people are upset, they do not talk about what is upsetting them; they attack.

In these situations of intense emotion, the therapist's first task is to help the client talk about the problem directly and calmly; verbal attacks have limited value. The therapist's task is to understand the environment of the client. To acquire this understanding, the therapist must be aware of what both he and the client are saying. He must note how embarrassing the problem is to the client, what both of them consider important or trivial, and what they both consider to be appropriate or inappropriate.

He must also note how the client reacts to what the therapist says. The therapist must know how to use language so that it can be informative, sympathetic, persuasive, manipulative or explorative. The therapy can easily flounder if the therapist's style of speaking to the client is inappropriate. The style varies as the content and the emotions of the situation change. The pacing and timing are part of the art of therapy. The therapist considers what can be said, how extensively a subject can be explored, and how long a particular focus can be maintained. The objective is to explore and understand without overwhelming the client.

RISK-TAKING

The ability and willingness to take risks in solving stress, threat and crisis emotions are measured by the amount of self the person in trouble is willing to invest in change. At the beginning of therapy, the client generally has little expectation that he can be effective in changing his situation. The client's ability or inability to take risks depends on past experience and the comparative degree of helplessness and hopelessness he sees in the present situation. The client will have an opinion as to the possibilities and opportunities that exist. Some sense of risk must be developed in the first interview, for if the client leaves without hope of change he may not return for a second session. This is often not easy, since the resolution of the problem may require that the client do something he dreads doing. It is in the task of risk-taking to achieve goals that the client's resistances are most easily seen, for the client often wants the therapist to take the responsibility. Responsibility implies performance, and the client would rather see the therapist perform — it is easier. The therapist must push the client, and the therapist can convey expectations to him in preparation for risk-taking — what the client can do, will do, should do.

WHAT, HOW AND WHY QUESTIONS

Determining the nature of the problem begins with a consideration of what happened and how it happened. A consideration of why it happened is generally not a proper focus of crisis therapy. "Why" questions often imply a hierarchy in the therapist-client relationship, for they assume that the therapist knows the right answer — and that the client is about to discover it. Failure to elicit the "correct" answer establishes the therapist as the superior person, and the client may perceive this as another form of rejection. "Why" questions imply guilt and responsibility, marking the therapist as a judge and thus increasing the client's anxiety. These "why" questions also locate the crisis within the client, thus raising his defenses and increasing depression. Placing location of the crisis outside the client, especially in the first interview, increases the possibility of coping.

FOCUS

Focus is an important feature of therapy. In determining what is relevant, which in turn determines what can feasibly be accomplished, the therapist follows the client's focus — but always with the purpose of avoiding subjects not directly related to the problem. The objective is to encourage the client to begin to see his situation as less risky, less unpredictable and less chaotic.

Conscious focus on the problem helps the therapist as well, for it discourages him from attempting to treat areas of personality malfunction that may become apparent, but that are not a proper focus for short-term therapy. Focus will reveal differences in the perception of the therapist and the client. This difference is based on the obvious but frequently overlooked fact that we perceive what we have learned to perceive, and what we want to perceive, when it fits into a pattern that has meaning based upon our experience.

Discovering what part of the client's understanding of his situation is correct and supports his functioning is especially important. Individuals of subgroups may have a realistic perception of their environment, but they may fail to understand which parts of their environment they can control, which support functioning and which do not. Members of subcultures often have unique perceptions of the reality of their situation that do not agree with the perceptions of the larger society. For example, violence is a normal part of life for some individuals.

CATHARSIS

In the initial interview, the client is likely to be overwhelmed by emotions and confusion. The interview is often a catharsis. By releasing his feelings, the client is attempting to explain the problem and to justify it, both to himself and to the therapist. The client may or may not question his own responsibility.

When a person is in stress, threat or crisis, his perception of the situation is limited. It focuses in only a few directions. As the story of the problem ("what happened") is told, the inconsistencies of the description begin to indicate the degree of the client's defense against the situation; it also indicates his degree of understanding. The therapist can point out these inconsistencies through questions and statements, such as: "What you just said does not agree with what you said before." One of the important aspects of this technique is that the therapist points out to the client, "I am listening to what you say — are you?" This must be done in a manner where the client comes to understand that the therapist's questions and challenges are not meant to offend, but instead they are intended to help.

The amount of time the client needs to complete the catharsis depends upon the intensity of his experience. The therapist learns through experience to judge when catharsis is appropriate and when it overwhelms the client. The therapist offers support in order to help the client accept his pain, and to realize that strong emotions are sometimes necessary to bring a sense of relief and safety.

When a repetitive pattern is noted, it must be broken, for here the client is merely discharging feelings and making no attempt to deal with the problem. These situations are difficult to handle and do not always occur during the first interview.

In catharsis the client often asks "why" questions: "Why did I?" "Why didn't I?" It is not necessary for the therapist to answer; the answer cannot be immediately determined. The client who asks such "why" questions is generally attempting to relieve some feeling of responsibility or guilt, or such questions may even be rhetorical in nature. The therapist who attempts to answer these questions often relieves too much responsibility or increases too much guilt.

EMOTION AND PAST EXPERIENCES

Emotion, which is expressed through affective qualities such as depression, anger, hopelessness or catharsis, is a manifestation of past and present consciousness memories and present encounters. Emotions, privately and consciously felt, result in tension. Tension does not necessarily mean conflict, but rather feeling which must be released to some degree.

In describing the problem, the client may relate his present situation to a previous experience. Such an experience may be similar to the present problem. The correlation between the two situations does not require the therapy to have an insight orientation. The experience of the situation itself can provide the insight. The client needs primarily to verbalize what he thinks and feels.

The therapist often makes the mistake of focusing on the client's previous problems. This begins the process of thinking about the past in reflective dependency, to understand the past. It consists of locating previous inadequacies without a consideration of the tasks to be undertaken now. It is not an appropriate focus for short-term therapy.

The therapist should listen to the client's story of the past in order to discover the theme for the present problem. Themes are not present in all problem situations, and some have more than one theme; if the themes can be determined, they can guide the therapist to clues as to how the problem has affected the client.

How the problem has affected the client is indicated by the intensity of the emotions. By considering the client's intensity, the therapist can begin to develop an understanding of what time frame is necessary to deal with the problem. The time frame, which is always an estimate, indicates the pacing of the therapy — the amount of time that should be allowed for a particular focus before an opportunity to develop a different focus is attempted.

One positive aspect of the intense emotions is that the client is emotionally accessible. The energy he has used to maintain his defenses has been shifted so that he is more susceptible to purposefully directed intervention.

DEFENSIVENESS

Not all people are prepared for or able to relate to a helping situation based on a dialogue. Therapy often requires the client to trust the therapist's statements, while his instinct leads him to suspect that the words are meant to mislead him. In therapy, words frequently express intensely charged feelings. The therapist should be aware of what words are being used; words can be neutral or provocative, clear or vague. For example, the therapist can tell someone who has an alcohol problem that he is an alcoholic — a negative label, or that alcoholism is a sickness. Or, the therapist can describe the situation as a general problem caused by drinking, or a health problem resulting from alcohol, or a personal habit of drinking that is out of control.

During the course of the interview, some individuals who mistrust the therapist may react with hostility. The situation may be frightening for the therapist. It should be anticipated that the individual in crisis may initially present problems that interfere with the assessment and the helping process. These problems often come from a lack of understanding and from confused emotion about both the problem and the delivery system.

The client, for example, may bring with him a fantasy of help based on what he wishes others to do to solve his problems, and if the help he imagines is not available or forthcoming, he may experience an intense feeling of loss. Or the client may be attempting to understand his problem by repeating the thoughts, feelings or behaviors associated with any or all aspects of the crisis. All this must be realistically acknowledged. The therapist should recognize the behaviors and feelings as a legitimate but unconstructive response to be overcome in order to get at the real problem.

A CASE EXAMPLE OF
THE FANTASY OF HELP

Louise was a 28-year-old white married woman

who was expecting a baby. She went to the local Planned Parenthood clinic to inquire about the possibility of having a test that would show what her baby was going to look like. The interview revealed that she had been married for eight years, that she loved her husband and wished to continue the marriage, although the couple did have some difficulties.

Her real problem was that she knew that this pregnancy, her first one, had resulted from her liaison with a black boyfriend. She wished to have a test that would tell her what color the baby would be and what characteristics it would have. The threat that underlay her crisis was that to have a black baby would ruin her marriage. To have an abortion might mean that she would lose every possibility of having her own child.

After the reason for Louise's request had been determined, the problem became one of deciding whether she should have an abortion. For our purposes, the important consideration in this case is that the presenting problem — a test to determine the unborn child's characteristics — was treated as legitimate. The reason for Louise's request was determined and the case proceeded from that point.

Resistance is a behavior that supports self-deception; it is often the client's way of coping with a problem. Although a crisis weakens defenses, the client may continue to maintain his self-deception by refusing to examine his involvement in the situation. That is, he may deny responsibility for, or even refuse to recognize the existence of, the basic problem.

In therapy, defenses are not considered pathological, but they are simply mechanisms by which the client avoids recognition of the problem. They provide a way for the client to reject help at the time he asks for it, thus contributing to a circular crisis state. This self-defensive but self-destructive attempt to avoid recognizing the problem results in part from a fear of the unknown — which could be the service system, the therapist or new ways of thinking. These are as frightening as new behaviors and experiences.

Defenses in crisis situations can consist of:

Behavior	Thought	Feelings
Hyperactivity	Frequent *change* in *focus*, but repetitive thoughts	Lack of awareness of others
Temper outbursts	Frequent and abrupt changes in thought	Despair: cannot be understood
Frequent and abrupt behavior changes	Refusal to listen or respond to the therapist	Feelings of persecution
Demands		Frequent and abrupt mood changes
Physical assaults		Demanding

RESPITE AND CRISIS

One of the important features of short-term and one-time therapy sessions is that the client, by describing his problem to the therapist — who then also thinks and talks about it — actually gets a rest from the pressures of the situation. This is referred to as respite.

Respite is as important to coping as problem-solving is to productive therapy. Indeed, the assumption that people who seek professional help during stress, threat or crisis do so with the goal of solving the problem is an assumption that belongs to the philosophical orientation of the professions; the client himself may only desire relief from his problem. The one-time interview can provide release from pressure and can give the client some perspective; and this may be all that the client desires, although it is not all he may need.

Other forms of respite people use in coping with stress are eating favored foods, shopping, taking a vacation, changing their residence, changing their associates, developing other interests such as sports or cultural or family affairs. The culturally-approved forms of respite are often overlooked in crisis therapy, but they are legitimate behaviors which can enable the client to cope. People of less sophistication and with fewer resources are more prone to crisis in part because they are less likely to seek and use culturally accepted forms of respite; they are more likely to encounter stress from which there is little rest.

Two other forms of respite commonly used in this culture are the use of alcohol and the use of legal or illegal drugs. These forms are popular because their effects are immediate, but in the long run they generally become part of the stress situation.

For those people who come for crisis counseling primarily to obtain respite, the door of the service system must always remain open. These are people whose stress so often becomes unmanageable, or appears to them to be unmanageable, during the hours when the crisis service is closed. These people are often chronic users of crisis services, and they become most unpopular with the helping staff because of their demands upon the service system and because of their inability to become successful cases.

It is true these can be difficult and tiresome cases, but it remains the province of the client to determine what type of service he requires and how much of it he needs to maintain his at-risk functioning, for that is all some people want. If service is denied to these people because they drop out frequently, or because of the chronic nature of their problems, then they can only obtain a service if they become sick physically or mentally, or are demanding and aggressive, or if they are brought to the attention of the police.

For many of these chronic clients, some service systems are really performing the service of people-sitting. There is little the service system can do for such clients, and there is little they are willing to do for themselves. Like small children, they are pushing the service system to do something for them, but whatever is done is not what they want. They can do nothing because they believe nothing can be done — even though they may wish to improve. The service system holds their hand until the intensity of the problem has passed.

These clients suffer from what is called chronic crisis. The crisis therapy described here may not be the treatment of choice since chronic crisis is generally not a decisive turning point for the sufferer, but rather an exacerbation, a continuing problem in a life whose normal pattern is a succession of problems.

Chronic users who seek respite but who don't improve are a constant problem for crisis services. It is particularly apparent in crisis services which maintain telephone hot lines. Their chronic consumers are people who call frequently to present problems, and who often call at particular times. These are sometimes problems which the service considers inappropriate for a crisis service. But the staff of the crisis services often fail to realize that the telephone call has saved the chronic respite-seeker a trip to the crisis center, with all the details of preparation, transportation and procedure involved.

Generally the caller believes his problem can be handled over the phone. But, more important, the caller gets the immediate attention of the helping person. It must also be recognized that a telephone interview is all the closeness and personal interaction that some people can tolerate. The caller can also use the telephone to control the helping person while remaining anonymous: the caller is able to discontinue the call when it is convenient to him, while the helping person feels obligated not to hang up. This is a frustrating experience for many helping people, since they are used to having control of the interviewing session. The helping person's anger is generally expressed in this situation when he indicates that the chronic caller is tying up telephone lines when there is probably someone with a "real crisis" trying to get through. This may be true, but the real problem may equally be that the helping person is not skilled in the use of the telephone as a means to therapy.

If the helping person on the crisis hot line does not talk with the lonely and troubled person, who will? The hot line may be one of the most neglected forms of preventive intervention.

THE CAPTIVE AND INVOLUNTARY CLIENT

Dealing with the captive and the involuntary client in public services often requires the skills of case management rather than of crisis therapy. Crises are composed of stress and threat, but not all situations of stress and threat are crises.

A distinction needs to be made between crisis, as previously defined, and stressful situations and emergencies which are experienced in the management of case problems. Such problems are often encountered with the involuntary client, on probation or parole, as well as with the captive client who has little choice of what service he receives — the client on public welfare. With some involuntary or captive clients, crisis is often the result of a lifestyle based on marginal coping; the crisis results from playing the odds.

Many such clients have experienced failures which have left them with little sense of competence. They have little, if any, expectation of achieving a sense of competence by participating in a helping service, and until the staff person proves to be helpful in some way, they will have no feeling of trust in the staff or the situation. Instead, they will see the encounter with the service delivery system as a new source of stress. It is stressful for the captive client in that the service may be denied him, and stressful for the involuntary client because he sees it as punishment for a problem. They must cope with the stress and threats of a system of which they have limited understanding. Therefore, what appears to be a crisis to the staff is often the overt, hostile, physical and verbal response of the client to the experience of the service system itself. It is these situations that are more truly problems of case management than of crisis intervention. Crisis with these clients deserves special consideration because of their unique features.

Often what is described as crisis within these service systems is a result of stress and threat both from the client's life and from the service system itself. These situations call for the staff's management of the stress which the client experiences from the service system before it results in a crisis.

The first realization must be that although the individual may not want to be a client of the service system, it is still, nevertheless, the individual and not the service system or the professional who is first of all responsible for his situation. However, we tend to exclude the client from the decision-making process which affects his life. This is done under the rationale that we are providing what is necessary for his security; the individual himself is considered incapable of handling these decisions.

In some cases, this is true. Generally, however, the person is excluded from the decision-making process because the service system is providing for its own comfort and security. Again, this can be necessary in some instances, but to take away all the control from the individual excludes him from becoming an active participant in a process that concerns his own life and future. This exposes the person to the constant stress of not knowing who makes the decisions about his life, or what the decision is based on. To be always at the mercy of mostly faceless strangers makes the client helpless and dependent. The ability to cope with this sort of stress is more than many people can tolerate. It is an artificial and dangerous situation which often leads to *"crisis."* To avert these situations requires that the client have the necessary information to begin to understand and anticipate the process in which he is involved. These stress situations can be summarized:

Needs of the client	*versus*	Needs of the service system
Limitations of the client	*versus*	Limitations of the service system
Resources of the client	*versus*	Resources of the service system

CRISIS AND AGGRESSION

In situations where the client indicates that he is not immediately willing or able to control his behavior — either physical or verbal — he is a threat both to himself and to the staff. The staff will fear the client's lack of control more than he will. This situation calls for active management. The client has to calm down either through talking or by exercise of demands and restraints. The situation can become an emergency when physical violence is threatened to the staff. ("Emergency" as used here means a sudden and generally unexpected occurrence or set of circumstances demanding immediate action.)

Confrontation and demand are tactics which some clients and groups have assumed; it takes energy and nerve to work with this type of client. Generally the staff wishes only to neutralize the situations of confrontation and demand. This is an appropriate response, but techniques which confront can also be appropriate. Often these situations are handled through the use of security guards or police. However, the use of such strong authority figures will often confront and escalate the situation at the same time. Aggressive tactics are difficult to deal with and often place the service system in what the staff members may feel to be their own crisis because of the demands and the responsibility involved.

No matter how these situations are resolved, they generally leave the staff with a sense of failure. That the staff may have failed may be true, but often the failure results from the staff's own fear of the situation, from their lack of awareness of what they think about aggression, and from negative feelings toward clients who engage in personal violence.

Situations of confrontation and demand are often complicated further by the service system's failure to have a policy that can guide staff as to what they may or may not do. If no policy states when to avoid the situation and when to challenge it, staff members find themselves in situations where the constraints are not clear; they often make the mistake of defending themselves by telling the client that they do not make the policies. This only serves to defeat the staff member and the service system, for the staff member will then be considered an obstacle to be pushed aside. The problem is only escalated. Clients often goad the staff member to see if he backs up what he says with conviction and if he will reject the client because of the client's confrontation tactics.

The staff must adhere to established principle of accepting the person — but not his negative behavior.

Confrontation is really a test between client and staff as to who has the greatest power to retaliate and who has the most to lose in the situation. Here the captive and involuntary client may have the advantage, because many such clients feel that they have nothing more to lose, that their attacks are fully justified. The clients may belong to a subculture which accepts violence as a means of expression and self-defense.

The staff person must understand clearly how much the client's negative behavior is controlling his own responses. Often the staff person will respond to confrontation with confusion and embarrassment. He will attempt to escape the situation and the rules which have provoked the confrontation. When a staff person feels trapped or frightened, he is in a situation of threat, and the anxiety or fear which results can determine his response. He is likely to fail to make a cognitive evaluation of the situation.

In crisis situations which are frightening or immediate, the helping person may feel robbed of his professional identity. He has been trained to help, and here the client is defeating his professional purpose and taking away his professional abilities. The result is a feeling of helplessness which may place the therapist in his own state of crisis. However, these are generally situations where the case was never managed from the beginning.

Management in these situations is an educational process during which it becomes clear what the individual can or cannot do, and what he can expect; these aspects concern the roles he can play which are relevant to the service system. At the same time, this educational process points out what the staff can do and how long it will take, or what it cannot do; these aspects of the situation at hand concern the role functions of the staff as they are predetermined by the service system.

Understanding of these basic facts through pacing and giving information, and repeating that information, is necessary to continue action.

This process gives a degree of responsibility to the individual for his actions and behavior, as well as the degree of autonomy he can exercise and a sense of time which operates within the system. If the client thinks that plans will be formulated and decisions will be made without his involvement, then the service delivery system is a constant stress because of this unknown.

Case management should reduce the stress resulting from confusion, conflicting messages and the transactions which the client and the staff must make. These situations are exacerbated when many staff members have not thought through their responsibility to the captive and involuntary client

— and to the service system. If the same staff of the same service system is asked to describe what they see themselves doing — not what the official job description says they do — the answers will vary: psychotherapy, casework, counseling, rehabilitation, reeducation, guidance. The individual staff member may be clear as to what his answer means to him, but the answers are words which have different meanings to different people. As a whole, the staff's concept of what it is doing with and for the clients varies among the staff members and may not be in agreement with the official policy of the service system. This lack of clarity about what is actually going on places yet another stress on the client: It makes the service system more difficult to understand. The situation is made still worse when clients are transferred from one staff member to another.

In many systems dealing with the captive and involuntary client, the nature, purpose and responsibility of the relationship is often vague and undefined to everyone involved. The staff person is often not sure what he is attempting to do and how he will achieve his goals, and the goals are generally set without consultation with the client. The client may not have the desire or the ability to achieve the goals set for him, and the staff member may not realize it. Nor is there a consideration of what social support systems exist to help the client achieve the goal.

The client will generally see the goal imposed on him as an imposition by an authority system which he does not like in the first place. In such a case, the staff and the client are doomed to failure — failure which will result in anger and in emergencies called *"crisis."*

ROLES OF THE THERAPIST

The therapist can assume a number of roles, all of which can change as the therapy progresses. Although none of them is neutral, they all require objectivity.

The therapist has a responsibility to perceive the client's problem in the broadest context. He must interpret reality in terms of the situational constraints, must support active coping, and must discourage passivity. The therapist legitimizes the problem by helping to define it; he expands resources by suggesting new ideas and strategies; he facilitates functioning by providing new information; and he develops, with the client, a strategy for resolution. The therapist can *mediate* between the person and his situation; he can be an *advocate* of action.

The person in crisis has three interrelated tasks:

1. To deal with the objective situation so as to reduce or eliminate its stressful characteristics (cognitive task).

2. To master the tensions and negative emotions which the crisis has created in him (affective task). This may be the primary task.
3. To confront other problems that have been created by the crisis and by previous coping efforts (situational task).

The therapist must understand the situation and must organize it in his mind so that what needs to be done and what can be done become clear. The tasks required of the client, their purpose and what they entail must also be made clear.

Throughout the therapy process, the client is being prepared and supported to do something about his situation. What he is willing and what he is able to do depends upon his readiness. Readiness for action is judged by:

1. The manner in which the client complains,
2. What he complains about,
3. Whether he listens to himself and to the therapist,
4. Whether he begins to classify and order what has happened.

The supportive techniques of therapy attempt to control the client's emotions so that he can begin to understand and solve his problem. The supportive techniques include reassurance, catharsis, education and suggestion. The techniques are used throughout the therapy, although some are more appropriate at particular times: catharsis in the initial interview, for example, and suggestion in setting goals for the future.

Reassurance, one of the most widely used techniques, is often rushed into without consideration of the damage that could result. There is a difference between reassurance based on the present ("We will work on your problem") and that based on the future ("You will be all right"). If reassurance is not based on present reality, it loses the vital quality of authenticity. The client, who often feels there is nothing positive about the situation, may see reassurance as a putdown since it can imply that the therapist either does not understand the situation or considers it insignificant. Gratuitous reassurance can increase guilt and add to depression.

The supportive-ventilating techniques of *catharsis* provide relief from tensions by means of emotional discharge. Catharsis often brings to conscious awareness important feelings and ideas about the situation, thus beginning the integration necessary to the problem-solving process. The therapist must control the ventilating process so that the client does not further frighten himself.

The *educational* aspect of crisis therapy provides support by making available information and knowledge about alternatives. The development of alternatives widens the client's perspective and gives him a sense of choice, which is important for mastery. This aspect of the treatment is directed toward the reestablishment of coping; the client can be educated (by the therapist, functioning as an advisor) to have psychological defenses.

Suggestion reinforces what the client can do, likes to do, needs to do, or is close to doing. It helps the client to expand his own resources, no matter how limited they may be.

Comments used in discussing the reality of the crisis situation may be *sympathetic*, in that they reflect what the client says and feels; they may *connect* what happened and how it happened; they may *sever links* by disposing of material not related to the crisis; they may enable the therapist to *confront* the client with his responsibilities, limitations or strengths; they may *facilitate*, by providing new information, awareness and development of coping strategies.

The therapist's comments should be made in words comprehensible to the client, words that are concrete and nonescalating. Their definition should be clear.

PROBLEM-SOLVING

Even though it does not set cure as a goal, crisis therapy does take a problem-solving approach. This does require time and it presents a difficulty for the person with a limited time-horizon.

In short-term treatment, problem-solving is a learning experience for the client. This does not mean that for every situation there is a clearly defined solution or a solution that will make everything all right. Most people have learned in school that for every problem a solution exists, and the solution is known only to the person in authority — the teacher (or the therapist). But this is not true in real life.

Preparing the client to become active in solving his problem begins with the first interview, since how quickly he improves correlates closely with the expectations the therapist conveys.

Resolving a crisis through a consideration of the problems that caused it reveals the importance of the educational aspect of therapy. The learning should be limited to the crisis problem: what happened, how it happened, and what can be done about the situation. Problem-solving requires a mutual decision as to what the client wants or needs and what can be done at the present time. This decision is influenced by the strategies that are available to the therapist and is generally contingent upon the policies and programs of the service system.

In problem-solving, a possible solution is developed that combines the client's abilities with the motivation of the crisis situation. However, the person in crisis is also in a state of ambivalence. Choosing a possible solution necessarily involves a consideration of the alternatives, and choosing among alternatives requires a decision and a risk. Even when it becomes clear to the client that a decision must be made, he will still want to know, "What can you do about it?" He is likely to think that only one solution can be right for all situations; he will want the therapist's approval.

The client must be led to discover and choose the solution. It is usually ineffective for the therapist to offer solutions. Generally, whatever the therapist offers the client will be rejected — unless it fits nicely into his motivational bases and/or his fantasy of what the service system can offer. If the client does accept the solution offered by the therapist, he will then expect the therapist to do all that is necessary to effect it, thus relieving him of any responsibility.

The therapist's main function is to assist the client in developing possible alternatives and in identifying the good and bad points of each alternative. Once a solution is decided upon and the steps involved are identified, the client should be supported and rewarded in the undertaking and completion of each step. If the client is not successful in completing the steps, the therapist has to determine at what step the process broke down. He must ask:

1. What is the problem, what are its limits, and which of its aspects are the most relevant at the time?
2. What are the present consequences of the problem?
3. What alternatives exist and what is the degree of risk for each alternative?
4. Which aspect of the problem can be immediately worked on with the greatest possibility of success?
5. What steps must the client take to resolve the problem?
6. What is the client's ability to accomplish each step?
7. What steps must the therapist take to aid in the process?

If the problem-solving breaks down, the task is not to determine compliance or noncompliance, but rather to develop another strategy. The failure of the client to implement successfully any predetermined strategy may mean that:

1. The predetermined strategy was not really "comfortable" for the client, possibly because he had little or no previous experience in using it; and/or
2. The important steps for that situation may not have been considered.

Determination of how accurately a predetermined strategy was implemented is not a proper focus for the therapist. What is important is how the client thinks he performed. Joy, apprehension or questioning indicate the degree of success that he feels. These qualities are conveyed not only in the words, but also by the manner in which they are expressed — fast, excited, reflective, inquisitive. It is important for the therapist to correlate words with the manner of presentation.

TERMINATION

In crisis therapy, termination is anticipated at the start, when the therapist begins to consider how long the crisis will take to run its course.

Termination can occur when the client has assumed the necessary control or has the necessary degree of competence to work with the problem. It is not necessary to wait until the entire problem has been solved, and the client can decide the time of termination himself. The therapist may not agree with the decision.

To what degree the behaviors and solutions are adaptive or maladaptive for the problem can be the primary consideration in making a decision to terminate. What is adaptive means what works for the client and has little possibility of causing another problem. Therefore, termination includes an evaluation called *anticipatory guidance*. This technique brings into conscious awareness which aspects of the problem have been resolved and which remain unresolved. Problems often have unfinished aspects, and the adaptive work necessary for anticipating future stress should be explored. Anticipatory guidance involves checking and planning for the immediate future; it includes preparation the client asks for or that the therapist thinks the client needs. It is not presented as something the client is instructed to follow. It is an educational technique intended to develop better understanding without producing anxiety.

During termination, the client should be informed of the possibility of future services. He can be encouraged to seek treatment from other sources for chronic problems. Termination should include a reinforcement of the positive adaptation and current functioning, but should not have the quality of finality.

GUIDELINES FOR THE THERAPIST

The guidelines for the therapist in crisis therapy can be summarized as follows:

1. The therapist represents authority, for he controls the therapy.

2. The focus is on the here-and-now. The therapist is aware and concerned about the everyday problems unless the focus is on future problems.

3. Goals are determined jointly. Such determination includes consideration of the steps necessary to reach a goal and the positive and negative outcomes.

4. The therapist should create a mutually sharing relationship by encouragement, trust and respect; he should use inclusive words such as "we," "our," "us." The intent is to reduce the tensions inherent in a relationship in which one person wields authority.

5. The therapist is a source of support and motivation for the client in the therapy process. The therapist should always be sincere. He should give the client his undivided attention. The therapist can express his own feelings and thoughts regarding the client's situation so that the client becomes better acquainted with him.

6. The therapist should be flexible in his approach in developing assessments and hypotheses. The client should be free to reject ideas and to accept those that appeal to him.
7. The therapist should work to reestablish the client's sense of identity and autonomy. Specific feedback and information should be given, and positive thinking and behavior should be reinforced.
8. The therapist acknowledges successful accomplishments of the client which the client considers to be satisfactory.

Operating procedures as they relate to the client are:

1. *The problem.* The problem that is causing the crisis must be defined. If the client is not able to define the problem by himself, it can be done jointly. The first definition of the problem does not have to be completely correct. The initial definition of the problem is designed to enable the client to relate his emotional state to some particular real situation. This begins the definition and redefinition of the problem.
2. *Responsibility.* In his description of the problem, does the client assume responsibility for his present situation? Has he attempted any activity to deal with the situation?

3. *Request.* Does the client have any ideas of the kind of service he wants and needs? Are they based upon fantasy or reality?

4. *Others.* Who or what in the problem situation helps or hinders the client?

5. *Background.* What has caused the client to ask for service now?

6. *Expectations.* What does the client expect of the therapy? Does he want an explanation, or does he want to be understood, valued, proved right? What can be offered must be clear. A passive approach on the part of the therapist will increase the client's expectation that when he stops talking, he will be given what he wants.

7. *Solutions.* What are the possible solutions to the problem? What are the steps involved? Every step must be considered, for the therapist does not know at what point the client will feel overwhelmed.

8. *Risk.* Is the client willing and able to take the risks required to reach a solution? The distinction between recognizing desires and carrying them out must be made clear. The client must be supported in assuming responsibility for some aspects of the problem.

CRISIS AND THE HEALTH PROFESSIONS

The health professionals who staff the acute and chronic care facilities are constantly confronted with situations of physical stress and threat which are multidimensional and often result in medical emergencies. These situations are resolved by medical and nursing staff. Their knowledge base and skill have become so sophisticated that physical equilibrium can often be reestablished and the emergency passes.

The development of the health professional into a highly-skilled practitioner has often left in a vacuum the emotional aspects attached to illness. Once the medical emergency has passed, the emotional stress of it, what it means, and how it affects the person, all have the potential for a crisis. Some illness and medical situations can be of such a magnitude that they affect every area of an individual's life. To cope with both the physiological and psychological stress and threat of illness is beyond the adjustive capacity of many individuals.

Situations of acute illness, the stress of incapacity, or chronic illness, require psycho-social coping to reestablish and maintain an emotional equilibrium. Without adequate coping, the situation may become a demoralizing experience which fosters maladaptive responses. Emotional coping with illness is a dynamic process which begins with diagnosis and changes with prognosis; each period adds different dimensions which requires a corresponding change in coping. The coping process with the emotional and physical aspects of the illness are not the patient's alone, but are also required of his family and friends.

The health professionals can be instrumental in helping the patient to develop coping skills if they see this as part of their role functioning. The health professional must consider that one of his roles is that of a teacher. The bedside manner has become one of bedside teaching so that the patient can begin to develop understanding of some aspect of his situation. As the patient understands or fails to understand, he will react physically, verbally and through affect, depression, anger — which graphically demonstrates his emotional coping. To become involved in this process requires that as the patient expresses his reaction, the health professional not fall back upon scientific knowledge and attempt to perform a task; it requires, in effect, that he does nothing except stand there and listen. It is the beginning of an involvement with the emotional aspects of the patient's coping.

Here the professional comes to know and understand what the situation means to the patient. However, the expertise of the health professional in providing skills has left him uncomfortable in assuming a teaching role which considers the emotional aspects of the individual's illness. The delivery of health care is an educational process in which the person is a responsible — not a passive — participant. The ultimate responsibility for coping with illness is the patient's — but he needs someone to help him begin and maintain the process.

To initiate the process of reestablishing coping generally begins with some information about the situation. To be physiologically helpless or impaired is a new situation and opens the door to feelings, thoughts and behaviors which may or may not be constructive, for the person does not know what is an appropriate form of coping and what is inappropriate.

People have different beliefs about accidents, sickness, pain, chronic disease and death which determine how they cope with the situation. Some individuals believe it to be a punishment or failure. Others must blame someone else or themselves. Belligerent, uncooperative and resistant behavior with the staff may be the result of anger based on thinking that it is the illness, not the person, that is the center of concern.

Patients often think their illness devalues them as a person. They do develop a deep awareness of the well, the sick, the chronically ill and the terminally ill.

Patients can also develop guilt about being a burden to their family or friends. The stress of this guilt is further complicated by feelings of self-pity and ambivalence over dependence and independence.

Providing a service to the physically ill requires balancing the physiological and psychological stresses. The professional's task-oriented work does not enable the person who is sick to begin to know the staff, nor does it allow the staff to begin to know the person. In these situations there is little opportunity for the patient to share feelings and the primary means of communication often takes the form of talking about the patient close enough so that he can hear — but without the explicit purpose of informing. This is accidentally done because the staff does not know what to tell the person, when to tell him, and whose responsibility it is to give him the information, that is, the doctor or the nurse.

Often in these situations no one takes the responsibility. What is overlooked is that there is little attempt to find out what the person already knows.

In other situations the knowledge which one staff has about the patient is not shared with the other staff; this results in a lack of team effort to understand and give attention to the emotional reactions. Patients do want to know how they are doing. They search the staff faces for any clue. If the staff is evasive especially through avoiding eye contact, the patient does not know how to interpret the situation.

It is also overlooked that many patients really find it difficult to explain what they are going through. Their explanation is often conveyed through affect; the well-intentioned but inappropriate cheery attitude by the staff can block the patient's response. The staff needs to feel comfortable in listening to the problems and feelings of the patient so that he is not further depressed. Without feeling comfortable, the anxiety or helplessness of the staff leads them to make reassurances which cannot be supported by the situation. This form of intervention only destroys the sense of trust; it does not listen to, attempt to understand or to inform the patient.

The education of the patient to cope with his situation does not call for long discussions of the disease processes. Instead it begins with the tasks which the health team performs: that is, the preparation of the patient beforehand so that he knows what to expect, development of some sense of understanding and therefore some mastery of the situation, reduction of the sense of helplessness and the state of tension which may lead to a crisis. When new procedures are started, the patient should know: how much discomfort to expect and for how long; whether the discomfort can be stopped to allow a rest if he thinks it is too much; what the procedure is and why it is being done.

It is difficult to either prepare the patient for pain or to understand his estimation of pain. A person in pain measures it against what he has previously experienced in life. It requires both physiological and psychological coping based on experience. Where experience with pain is limited, coping breaks down; this is manifested in depression.

For the health professional to intervene with the patient to help him cope with the situation through understanding and release of affect requires the professional's feeling comfortable in involvement with the problems of another person. In the reality of everyday work this means having the time, even five minutes, to look, listen, touch, talk, ask questions and to accept emotional reactions. The acceptance of an emotional reaction becomes the touchstone through which the stress of the situation can be partly lifted. However, emotions of sorrow are difficult to alleviate as opposed to anger, depression or guilt. To intervene with sorrow simply requires that someone have the time to listen so that the individual does not also feel isolated, and thereby begins to process the experience.

REFERENCES

1. Malan, D.H., *A Study of Brief Psychotherapy,* London, Tavistock Publications, 1963.
2. Reid, William J. and Shyne, Ann W., *Brief and Extended Casework,* New York, Columbia University Press, 1969.
3. Langsley, Flomenhaft and Machotla, "Follow-Up Evaluations of Family Crisis Therapy," *American Journal of Orthopsychiatry,* 1967.
4. Wood, M. Katherine, "Casework effectiveness: A New Look at the Research Evidence," *Journal of the National Association of Social Workers,* Vol. 23, #6, November, 1978, p. 451.

Author's Epilogue

LIVING IN TODAY'S society presents the average individual with a great deal of stress over which he has limited control. These stressful times are further complicated by uncertainty, in both the present and the future. The individual is often not sure where he is, where he is going, and how much control he has over his own life.

Every individual must cope with these stresses, but coping with stress which appears to be unending can lead to intense frustration. The stress of frustration can be overwhelming, for it can rob the individual of the vital coping ability of hope.

All of these problems, and many more, are happening every day in every human service delivery system. Crisis intervention services are encountering problems stemming from frustration, confusion and uncertainty. Clients are demanding and aggressive, and they do have complex and difficult problems in living.

The problem of our clients can also result in stressful times for the helping professions. But, as members of the helping professions, we must not become personally and professionally frustrated. If we lose the vital quality of hope, then we can offer little to the people who need our services the most.

Selected Readings

I. Theoretical Considerations

1. Aldrich, C. Knight: "Impact of Community Psychiatry on Casework and Psychotherapy," *Smith College Studies in Social Work*, Vol. 38, No. 2, February, 1968, pp. 102-115.
2. Bloom, Bernard: "Definitional Aspects of the Crisis Concept," *Journal of Consulting Psychology*, Vol. 27, No. 6, December, 1963, pp. 498-502.
3. Brenner, Harvey: "Economic Change and Mental Hospitalization: New York State, 1910-1960," *Social Psychiatry*, Vol. 9, No. 4, 1967, pp. 180-188.
4. __________: *Mental Illness and the Economy*. Cambridge, Mass., Harvard University Press, 1976.
5. Caplan, Gerald: (ed.) *The Prevention of Mental Disorders in Children*. New York, Basic Books, 1961.
6. Chu, Franklin and Trotter, Sharland: *The Madness Establishment*. Ralph Nader's Study Group Report on the National Institute of Mental Health. New York, Grossman Publishers, 1974.
7. Erikson, Erik: "Growth and Crises of the Healthy Personality," *Personality in Nature, Society, and Culture*, Clyde Kluckhohn, Henry A. Murray, and David M. Schneider (eds.), 2nd ed. revised and enlarged. New York, Alfred A. Knopf, 1953, Chapter 7. Also in *Psychological Issues*, Vol. 1, No. 1, 1959.
8. Golan, Naomi: "When Is a Client in Crisis?" *Social Casework*, Vol. 50, No. 7, July, 1969.
9. Halmos, Paul: *The Faith of the Counsellors*. New York, Schocken Books, 1966.
10. Hill, Reuben: "Generic Features of Families Under Stress," *Social Casework*, Vol. 39, Nos. 2-3, 1958.

11. Kalis, B.L., Harris, M.R., and Prestwood, A.R.: "Precipitating Stress as a Focus in Psychotherapy," *Archives of General Psychiatry*, Vol. 3, 1961, pp. 219-226.

12. Kaplan, David M.: "A Concept of Acute Situational Disorders," *Social Work*, Vol. 7, No. 2, April, 1962, pp. 15-23.

13. Kaplan, David M., and Mason, Edward: "Maternal Reaction to Premature Birth Viewed as an Acute Emotional Disorder," *American Journal of Orthopsychiatry*, Vol. 30, July, 1960, pp. 539-552.

14. Klein, D., and Lindemann, E.: "Preventive Intervention in Individual and Family Crisis Situations," in *Prevention of Mental Disorders in Children*, E. Caplan (ed.), New York, Basic Books, 1961.

15. Lazarus, Richard: *Psychological Stress and the Coping Process*. New York, McGraw-Hill, 1966.

16. Lindemann, Erich: "Symptomatology and Management of Acute Grief," *American Journal of Psychiatry*, September, 1944, Vol. 101.

17. _______: "The Psychosocial Position in Etiology," in Kruae, H.D., *Approaches to Mental Disease*, Harper, 1957.

18. Liefer, Ronald: *In the Name of Mental Health: the Social Functions of Psychiatry*. New York, Science House, 1969.

19. LeVine, Robert: *Culture, Behavior, and Personality*. Chicago, Adline Publishers, 1973.

20. Malan, D.H.: *A Study of Brief Psychotherapy*. London, Tavistock Publications, 1963.

21. Maslow, A.H.: *Motivation and Personality*. New York, Harper and Row, 1954.

22. Parad, Howard J.: (ed.) *Crisis Intervention: Selected Readings*. New York, Family Service Association of America, 1965.

23. Parad, Howard J., and Caplan, Gerald: "A Framework for Studying Families in Crisis," *Social Work*, Vol. 5, July, 1960.

24. Pelleiter, Kenneth: *Mind as Healer, Mind as Slayer.* New York, Dell Pub. Co., 1977.

25. Phillips, E.L., and Wiener, D.N.: *Short-term Psychotherapy and Structured Behavior Change.* New York, McGraw-Hill Book Co., 1966.

26. Rapoport, Lydia: "The State of Crisis: Some Theoretical Considerations," *The Social Service Review,* Vol. 36, No. 2, July, 1962.

27. Rapoport, Rona: "Normal Crises: Family Structure and Mental Health," *Family Process,* Vol. 2, 1963, pp. 68-80.

28. Rokeach, Milton: *Beliefs, Attitudes and Values: A Theory of Organization and Change.* San Francisco, Jossey-Bass, Inc., Pub., 1976.

29. Schulberg, H.D., and Sheldon, A.: "The Probability of Crisis and Strategies for Preventive Intervention," *Archives of General Psychiatry,* Vol. 18, May, 1968, pp. 553-558.

30. Selby, Lola G.: "Social Work and Crisis Theory," *Social Work Papers,* University of Southern California, Vol. 10, 1963.

31. Strean, H.S., and Blatt, A.: "Long or Short-term Therapy?" *Journal of Contemporary Psychotherapy,* Vol. 1, No. 2, Winter, 1969, pp. 115-122.

32. Taft, Jessie: *The Dynamics of Therapy in a Controlled Relationship.* New York, The Macmillan Co., 1933.

33. The President's Commission on Mental Health, 1978, Volume I, II, III, IV.

34. Tyhurst, James S.: "The Role of Transition States — Including Disasters — In Mental Illness," *Symposium on Preventive and Social Psychiatry,* Washington, D.C.: Walter Reed Army Institute of Research, 1957, pp. 149-159.

35. Wheelis, Allen: "The Place of Action in Personality Change," *Psychiatry,* May, 1950

II. Practice Applications

36. Bandler, Bernard: (eds.) Howard J. Parad and Roger R. Miller: "The Concept of Ego Supportive Psychotherapy," in *Ego Oriented Casework: Problems and Perspectives.*

37. Beck, Helen L.: *The Closed Short-term Group.* U.S. Department of Health, Education and Welfare, Children's Bureau, 1965.

38. Bellak, Leopold, and Small, Leonard: *Emergency Psychotherapy and Brief Psychotherapy.* New York, Grune and Stratton, 1965.

39. Coleman, M.D., and Zwerling, I.: "The Psychiatric Emergency Clinic: A Flexible Way of Meeting Community Mental Health Needs," *American Journal of Psychiatry,* Vol. 115, No. 11, May, 1959, pp. 980-984.

40. Elkin, Meyre: "Short-contact Counseling in a Conciliation Court," *Social Casework,* Vol. 43, No. 4, April, 1962.

41. Foeckler, Merle M.: "Dynamics of Coping With a Medical Crisis," *Public Welfare,* Vol. 23, Jan., 1965, pp. 41-46.

42. Forer, Bertram R.: "The Therapeutic Value of Crisis," *Psychological Reports,* Vol. 13, pp. 275-281.

43. Frings, John: "What About Brief Services?" *Social Casework,* Vol. 32, No. 6, June, 1951, pp. 236-242.

44. Goffman, Erving: "On Cooling the Mark Out," *Psychiatry: Journal for the Study of Interpersonal Process,* Vol. 15, No. 4, pp. 451-513.

45. Haley, Jay: "Control in Brief Psychotherapy," *Archives of General Psychiatry,* No. 4, February, 1961, pp. 139-154.

46. Hankoff, L.D.: *Emergency Psychiatric Treatment,* Springfield, Illinois, Charles, C. Thomas, 1969.

47. Jacobson, Gerald F.: "Crisis Theory and Treatment Strategy: Some Socio-Cultural and Psychodynamic Considerations," *Journal of Nervous and Mental Disease,* Vol. 141, No. 2, August, 1965.

48. Jacobson, Gerald F., et al.: "Generic and Individual Approaches to Crisis Intervention," *American Journal of Public Health*, Vol. 58, No. 2, February, 1968, pp. 338-343.

49. _________: "The Scope and Practice of an Early-Access Brief Treatment Psychiatric Center." *American Journal of Psychiatry*, Vol. 121, No. 12, June, 1965.

50. Kaffman, Mordecai: "Short-term Family Therapy," *Family Process*, Vol. 2, No. 2, September, 1963, pp. 216-234.

51. Kaplan, David M. "Observations on Crisis Theory and Practice," *Social Casework*, Vol. 49, No. 3, March, 1968, pp. 151-155.

52. Karp, H. Neil, and Karls, James M.: "Combining Crisis Therapy and Mental Health Consultation," *Archives of General Psychiatry*, Vol. 14, May, 1966, pp. 536-542.

53. Koeyler, Brill, Epstein and Forgy: "A Psychiatric Clinic Evaluates Brief Contact Therapy," *Mental Hospitals*, October, 1964.

54. Levine, Rachel: "A Short Story on the Long Waiting List," *Social Work*, Vol. 8, Jan., 1963, pp. 20-22.

55. Lowry, Fern: "Casework Principles for Guiding the Worker in Contacts of Short Duration," *Social Service Review*, Vol. 22, No. 2, June, 1948, pp. 234-239.

56. MacLeod, John A., and Middleman, Francine: "Wednesday Afternoon Clinic: A Supportive Care Program," *Archives of General Psychiatry*, Vol. 6, Jan., 1962, pp. 72-81.

57. Murray, Edward, and Smitson, Walter: "Brief Treatment of Parents in a Military Setting," *Social Work*, Vol. 8, No. 2, April, 1963.

58. Parad, Howard J.: "Brief Ego Oriented Casework with Families in Crisis," in *Ego Oriented Casework; Problems and Perspectives*, Howard J. Parad and Roger B. Miller (eds.), New York, Family Service Association of America, 1963.

59. Paul, Louis: "Crisis Intervention," *Mental Hygiene*, Vol. 50, No. 1, Jan., 1966.

60. Porter, Robert A.: "Crisis Intervention and Social Work Models," *Community Mental Health Journal*, Vols. 1 and 2, Spring, 1966.

61. Pumpian-Mindlin, E.: "Considerations in the Selection of Patients for Short Term Therapy," *American Journal of Psychotherapy*, Vol. 7, 1953.

62. Purcell, Francis: "The Helping Professions and Problems of Brief Contact in Low Income Areas," in *Mental Health of the Poor*, Reissman, Cohen, and Pearl (eds.), New York, Free Press, 1964.

63. Reid, William, and Epstein, Laura: (eds.) *Task-centered Practice*, New York, Columbia University Press, 1977.

64. Reid, William, and Shyne, Ann: *Brief and Extended Casework*, New York, Columbia University Press, 1969.

65. Rapoport, Lydia: "Working with Families in Crisis: An Exploration in Preventive Intervention," *Social Work*, Vol. 7, No. 3, July, 1962.

66. _________: "Crisis-oriented Short-term Treatment," *Social Service Review*, Vol. 41, No. 1, March, 1967.

67. Ryan, W.: *Blaming the Victim*, New York, Vintage Books, 1972.

68. Rosenbaum, C.P.: "Events of Early Therapy and Brief Treatment," *Archives of General Psychiatry*, Vol. 10, May, 1964, pp. 506-512.

69. Servis, Mary A., Dewees, S., and Johnson, R.: "A Concept of Ego Oriented Psychotherapy," *Psychiatry; Journal for Study of Interpersonal Processes*, Vol. 22, No. 3, August, 1959.

70. Shader, R.I., and Schwartz, A.J.: "Management of Reactions to Disaster," *Social Work*, Vol. 11, No. 2, April, 1966, pp. 99-104.

71. *Social Work Papers*, The School of Social Work, University of Southern California, Vol. 20, 1963. (Eight papers on crisis work).

72. Stevenson, I.: "Direct Instigation of Behavioral Changes in Psychotherapy," *AMA, Archives of General Psychology*, Vol. 1, 1959, pp. 99-107.

73. Strickler, Martin: "Applying Crisis Theory in a Community Clinic," *Social Casework*, Vol. 46, No. 3, March, 1965.

74. Strickler, Martin, et al.: "The Community-based Walk-in Center: A New Resource for Groups Underrepresented in Outpatient Treatment Facilities," *American Journal of Public Health*, Vol. 55, No. 3, March, 1965, pp. 377-384.

75. Strickler, Martin, and Allgeyer, Jean: "The Crisis Group: A New Application of Crisis Theory," *Social Work*, Vol. 12, No. 3, July, 1967.

76. Thomas, Dorothy: "Relationship Between Diagnostic Service and Short Contact Cases," *Social Casework*, Vol. 32, No. 2, February, 1951, pp. 74-81.

77. Townsend, Gladys: "Short Term Casework with Clients Under Stress," *Social Casework*, Vol. 34, No. 9, November, 1953, pp. 392-398.

78. Tulane University School of Social Work, *Proceedings of Workshop in Influencing the Positive Use of Crisis*, New Orleans, Louisiana, February, 1962.

79. Wolberg, Lewis R.: *Short-term Psychotherapy*. New York and London, Grune and Stratton, 1965.

III. Research Perspectives

80. Avnet, Helen H.: "How Effective Is Short-term Therapy?" in *Short Term Psychotherapy*, Lewis R. Wolbert (ed.), New York, Grune and Stratton, 1965, pp. 7-22.

81. Beck, Dorothy F.: *Patterns in Use of Family Agency Service*. New York, Family Service Association of America, 1962.

82. Berkman, P.: "Measurement of Mental Health in a General Population Survey," *American Journal of Epidemiology*, 94, 105-111, 1971.

83. Bergin, Allen, E.: "Some Implications of Psychotherapy Research for Therapeutic Practice," *International Journal of Psychiatry*, Vol. 3, March, 1967, pp. 136-150.

84. Blenker, Margaret, et al.: *Serving the Aging.* New York, Community Service Society of New York, 1964.

85. Briar, Scott: "Family Service," in *Five Fields of Social Service: Reviews of Research*, Henry S. Mass (ed.), New York, National Association of Social Workers, 1966, pp. 9-50.

86. Bloom, Bernard: "Definitional Aspects of the Crisis Concept," *Journal of Consulting Psychology*, Vol. 27, No. 6, December, 1963, pp. 498-502.

87. Caplan, Gerald, et al.: "Four Studies of Crisis in Parents of Prematures," *Community Mental Health Journal*, Vol. 1, Summer, 1965, pp. 149-161.

88. Darbonne, Allen: "Crisis: A Review of Theory, Practice, and Research." *International Journal of Psychiatry*, Vol. 6, No. 5, November, 1968, pp. 371-379. See also discussions by Bloom and Farberow, pp. 380-384.

89. Duckworth, Grace: "A Project in Crisis Intervention," *Social Casework*, Vol. 38, No. 4, April, 1967, pp. 227-231.

90. Eysenck, Hans J.: *The Effects of Psychotherapy.* New York, International Science Press, 1966.

91. Frank, Jerome D.: *Persuasion and Healing.* New York, Schocken Books, 1965.

92. Garcea, Ralph A., and Irwin, Olive: "A Family Agency Deals with the Problem of Drop-Outs," *Social Casework*, Vol. 43, February, 1962, pp. 71-75.

93. Gilbert, Anita: "An Experiment in Brief Treatment of Parents," *Social Work*, Vol. 5, October, 1960, pp. 91-97.

94. Herzog, Elizabeth: *Some Guidelines for Evaluative Research.* US Department of Health, Education and Welfare, Children's Bureau, Washington, D.C., 1959.

95. Janis, Irving: *Psychological Stress.* New York, Wiley and Sons, 1958.

96. Kogan, Leonard S.: "The Short-term Case in a Family Agency," Parts I, II, and III, *Social Casework*, Vol. 38, Nos. 5, 6 and 7, May, June and July, 1957.

97. Malan, D.H. *A Study of Brief Psychotherapy.* Springfield, Illinois, Charles C. Thomas, 1963.

98. Parad, Howard J., and Parad, Libbie G.: "A Study of Crisis-Oriented Planned Short-term Treatment," Part I, *Social Casework*, Vol. 49, June, 1968, pp. 345-355.

99. _________: "A Study of Crisis-Oriented Planned Short-term Treatment," Part II, *Social Casework*, Vol. 49, July 1968, pp. 418-626.

100. Phillips, E. Lakin, and Johnston, Margaret S.: "Theoretical and Clinical Aspects of Short-term Parent-child Psychotherapy," *Psychiatry*, Vol. 17, August, 1954, pp. 267-275.

101. Reid, William J., and Shyne, Ann W.: *Brief and Extended Casework.* New York, Columbia University Press, 1969.

102. Reynolds, Bertha C.: "An Experiment in Short-contract Interviewing," Smith College Studies in *Social Work*, Vol. 3, September, 1932, pp. 3-107.

103. Shaw, Robert, et al.: "A Short-term Treatment Program in a Child Guidance Clinic," *Social Work*, Vol. 13, No. 3, 1968, pp. 81-90.

104. Shlien, J.M.: "Cross-theoretical Criteria in Time-limited Therapy," Proceedings of the Sixth International Congress of Psychotherapy, London, 1964, Part IV. Basel/New York, S. Karger, 1965, pp. 118-126.

105. Shyne, Ann: "What Research Tells Us About Short-term Cases in Family Agencies," *Social Casework*, Vol. 38, No. 5, May, 1957, pp. 223-231.

106. Stoller, Frederick H.: "Accelerated Interaction: A Time-limited Approach Based on the Brief Intensive Group," mimeo report, State of California Department of Mental Hygiene, Bureau of Research, March, 1966.

107. Sullivan, P., Miller, C., and Smelser, W.: "Factors in Length of Stay and Progress in Psychotherapy," *Journal of Consulting Psychology*, Vol. 22, No. 1, 1958.

108. Ungerleider, J. Thomas: "The Psychiatric Emergencies," *Archives of General Psychiatry*, Vol. 3, December, 1960, pp. 593-601.

Appendix

109. Szasz, Thomas: *The Ethics of Psychoanalysis: the Theory and Method of Autonomous Psychotherapy.* New York, Basic Books, 1965.

110. _________: *The Manufacture of Madness.* New York, Harper and Row, 1977.

BIBLIOGRAPHY ADDENDUM

THEORETICAL CONSIDERATIONS

111. Nevitt, Sanford: *Issues in Personality Theory.* San Francisco, Jossey-Bass, Inc., 1970.

112. Phillips, Derek L.: *Rejection: A Possible Consequence of Seeking Help for Mental Disorders,* Amen. Social Rev. 28: 913-972 (Dec.), 1963, p. 965.

113. Erwing, Coffman: *Asylums: Essays on the Social Situation of Mental Patients and other Inmates.* New York, Anchor Books, 1961.

PRACTICE APPLICATIONS

114. Fecel, Allan B., and Levenson, Alan I.: *The Community Mental Health Center: Strategies and Programs.* New York, Basic Books, 1972.

115. Lieb, Julian, Lipstich, Ian I., and Andrew, Edmund Slaby: *The Crisis Team: A Handbook for the Mental Health Professional.* New York, Harper & Row, 1973.

116. Baker, Frank: "From Community Mental Health to Human Service Ideology," *American Journal of Public Health,* June, 1974, Vol. 64, No. 6, pp. 576-580.

117. Philip, R.A., May, M.D., and Cohen, Jerome, Ph.D.: "Development Operations in Mental Health Delivery Systems," *American Journal of Public Health,* February, 1975, Vol. 5, No. 2, pp. 156-162.

118. Gross, Marion L.: *The Psychological Society.* New York, Random House, 1978.

119. Rabkin, Judith, and Struening, Elder L.: Working Paper Series No. 17, Ethnicity, *Social Class and Mental Illness,* Institute on Pluralism and Group Identity.

RECENT MATERIALS

Kliman, Ann S.: *Psychological First Aid for Recovery and Growth.* New York, Holt, Rinehart and Winston, 1978.

Lamb, H. Richard: (ed.) *Alternatives to Acute Hospitalization.* San Francisco, Jossey-Bass, 1979.

Dixon, Samuel L.: *Working with People in Crisis: Theory and Practice.* St. Louis, Mosby, 1979.

Small, Leonard: *The Briefer Psychotherapies.* New York, Brunner/Mazel, 1979.

"Crisis Intervention Centers: A Study of Available Services: Report of the Subcommittee on Crisis Intervention Centers." The General Assembly, Hartford, Connecticut (undated).

Wicks, Robert J., Fine, Jeffrey A., Platt, Jerome J.: (eds.) *Crisis Intervention: A Practical Clinical Guide.* New York, C.B. Slack, 1979.

Rueveni, Uri: *Networking Families in Crisis: Intervention Strategies with Families and Social Networks.* New York, Human Sciences Press, 1979.

Golan, Naome: *Treatment in Crisis Situations.* New York, The Free Press, 1978.

Ewing, Charles Patrick: *Crisis Intervention as Psychotherapy.* New York, Oxford University Press, 1978.

Hoff, Lee Ann: *People in Crisis: Understanding and Helping.* Menlo Park, Calif., Addison-Wesley Pub. Co., 1978.

Smith, Larry Lorenzo: *Crisis Intervention Theory and Practice: A Source Book.* Washington, D.C., University Press of America, 1976.

Whitlock, Glenn E.: *Understanding and Coping with Real-Life Crises.* Monterey, Calif., Brooks/Cole Pub. Co., 1978.

Nass, Stanley: (ed.) *Crisis Intervention.* Dubuque, Iowa, Kendall/Hunt Pub. Co., 1977.

Crow, Gary A.: *Crisis Intervention.* New York, Association Press, 1977.

Lindsay-Nedlands, Rae: *Crisis Theory: A Critical Overview.* University of Western Australia Press, 1975.

Calhoun, Lawrence G., Selby, James W., and King, H. Elizabeth: *Dealing with Crisis: A Guide to Critical Life Problems.* Englewood Cliffs, New Jersey, Prentice Hall, 1976.